CONDOR JOURNAL

CONDOR JOURNAL

The History, Mythology and Reality of the California Condor

DICK SMITH
Olive Kingston Smith, editor

Co-published by Capra Press and the
Santa Barbara Museum of Natural History
1978

To the California Condor. The majesty of the primitive ages is in him as he comes winging out of the ice age, the majesty of the silences that were before man and will perhaps be after him.

—*DICK SMITH*

Library of Congress Cataloging in Publication Data

Smith, Richard Jay, 1920-1977.
   Condor journal.

   "California condor (revised and updated from the 1964 edition": p.
   Bibliography: p.
   Includes index.
   1. California condor.   I. Smith, Richard Jay, 1920-1977. California
condor.   II. Title.
QL696.F33S62   1978   598.9'1   77-28243
ISBN 0-88496-080-3

CAPRA PRESS
631 State Street, Santa Barbara, California 93101

CONTENTS

DICK SMITH:
"CONSCIENCE OF THE COUNTY"

He came to California back in 1948 with a trunkful of tools and a change of clothes. He bought a house in Summerland and in a frenzied burst of skill and energy, rebuilt it from stem to stern within a month, in time for the arrival of his pregnant wife and two infant daughters.

Six months later we bought a goatshed together on a piece of rolling grassland on the northern edge of Santa Barbara and built two houses, using his tools. We put in windows framing the Santa Ynez mountains—windows that stared at La Cumbre lookout which commanded access to the mysterious backcountry.

Dick's energy was prodigious. After a day's work as staff artist at the News-Press, he was back to his land with a jeepload of salvaged lumber. Time to gulp dinner and grab his hammer. He seemed inexhaustible. At midnight he'd make popovers and tell stories of the Minnesota northcountry where he tramped in his youth—tales set in Norwegian pines, lily swamps and beaver dams. One night he brought home a story of California's Hurricane Deck where lions roamed and condors soared. "We're going there," he said, "soon as this house is done."

Two years later we drove up Figueroa Mountain to fill sacks with pine cones to christen his stone fireplace. We stared out at the San Rafael Mountains and Dick tried to identify the Deck from the roadmap in his hand. Looking out over that vast wild land, wind pushing through the Ponderosas overhead, Dick was struck dumb. He saw a distant bird—condor, eagle, or hawk we couldn't know—and stretched out his arm as though laying claim then and there.

7

As the sun sank we climbed to the fire lookout where a light burned in the window. As we came near we saw the ranger hunched down feeding his dogs. Seeing us they melted into the shadows and the ranger came forward testily wondering what we wanted. Dick said he'd like to know how to get into Hurricane Deck and hoped he hadn't disturbed the dogs.

"Those weren't dogs you scared off," the ranger said. "That was mama fox with her two new pups. She doesn't trust strangers but she'll eat out of my hand." Dick's kind of man.

That opened a two-hour conversation ending inside the lookout bent over the map table. Dick traced the shape of Hurricane Deck on a scrap of paper and stuffed it into his pocket.

The ranger was an older man, lame and unable to move through the backcountry anymore. "There's hidden trails down in there that lead to secret springs, painted caves and five-fingered ferns. It's moon country in some places but still you'll find paradise meadows with flowers like you've never seen. If you go in, be an animal and don't leave a human sign. If you care to bother, come back and tell me what you find."

Dick pledged he would and I believe his first trips into the backcountry were on behalf of that fox-feeding ranger. After that, he couldn't be kept away. His house was done (as done as it would ever be, though he kept rebuilding it over the years) and nothing could stop him.

Most of his first trips were on foot, but he soon found that hiking hampered his range since he rarely could be away more than two days, so he bought a good trail horse, built her a saddle to fit like a glove, and on that mare his penetrations into the backcountry got deeper and to the heart.

In the early years condors were incidental. His interest focused keenly on Indian caves and remains of nineteenth century home-steads (signaled sometimes by a gnarled apple tree rising from the chaparral, bearing fruit he harvested and ate). His view was both panoramic and minute, absorbed as much in a mountain range as in the hang of pollen on the bloom of a small flower. Occasionally, a great winged shadow crossed over the lone figure of Dick Smith as he trudged up a godforsaken slope. How landbound it made him feel, to see a condor glide effortlessly over that convoluted land without a motion of its wings, to move across the entire sky in a matter of minutes while it had taken him all morning to move up the mountain a few miserable miles. That was enough to wed Dick to the glory of that bird and the frailty of man.

Though Dick went often alone, he usually sought company of people who at least in some small measure shared the heart response. In this way he was utterly selfless, a prophet to those who would listen. He knew the lore of plants, animals and birds more intimately than anyone before him. He passed it on to his children, friends and public audiences, wrote books, articles and gave talks—a man who had at least three lifetimes rolled into a single body. That's why some say he was over 150 years old on February 2, 1977 when he died feeding his horses 56 years after he was born.

For him it wasn't enough to build a house (and nearly everything in it), raise a family (three daughters and a son), and make a career of newspaper work. Drawing from energies beyond our ken, he became the "conscience of our county," learning more in his 30 years here than a century of people before him had learned about backcountry and islands, city affairs, and husbandry on the valley ranches. Besides this, he wrote two other books, "California's Back Country" and "Beachwalkers Guide" and delivered endless talks and slide shows at the Museum of Natural History and other audiences. His nature photography was frequently exhibited, his annual sketches of the 4-H Fair filled pages of the Sunday paper, his testimony as an environmentalist in Washington and Sacramento had influence on wilderness legislation and brought him commendation in the Congressional Record. In 1977 the County Trails Council installed a memorial plaque dedicating the Jesusita Trail to Dick Smith. A proposal to expand the San Rafael Wilderness Area in his name and memory is now being considered.

His activities were never enough. He designed and built a small sailboat, hewed the mast, carved the rudder, molded the hull and sewed the sails; Christmastime he made things for friends—fireplace bellows one year, framed slabs of stone with facsimile cave paintings the next, carved shore birds. Imagine making ten bellows from hide he tanned, wood he carved and copper he pounded.

His relentless vision drove him through the slow, ungainly machinations of organizations and government bodies, always seeking out individuals within these groups he might inspire. And though they might be slow to understand and lagging in action, one thought prevailed in Dick's mind—KEEP THE WILDERNESS WILD. He would say we must have a treaty with nature if we are to survive. If we plunder our environment of its last spark of life, the planet will die under our feet.

For example, strip mining in the Sespe (threatening one of the last condor nesting sites) for phosphates to be rendered into detergents, Dick saw as an outrage. Not that the condor is directly useful to man, but that the whole scheme of nature which provides us with clean air and water and tolerable climate must be kept in equilibrium. The existence of the condor he regarded as a symptom of the ultimate health and well-being of the only world we have to live on. Everything matters in its natural state, from the smallest creatures that creep and crawl to the great soaring condor. Of course, man needs to wash his clothes, but not at the expense of a wild canyon which in its original state affects the weather, watershed, oxygen and a thousand other subtle qualities of life such as silence and sanctuary. People can find other ways of doing their laundry.

Dick's ceaseless searching through the backcountry for signs of another age, when Indians lived in apparent harmony with the hills, rewarded him with cave paintings to puzzle over, interpret and through them to divine a more natural way of life. This may also explain his fascination with homestead ruins, suggesting a time when a few people laid claim to land that wasn't ordained to be theirs. And perhaps that's why, high above all else, he saw the condor sweeping across the sky as the grandest symbol of natural continuity—a bird from the Pleistocene surviving into this age of airlines.

—NOEL YOUNG

Part I

FIELD JOURNAL: 1964-1977

FOREWORD

This journal section was conceived on a downtown sidewalk during a noon hour in October 1976. Dick came loping up, hugged me triumphantly and made the incredible announcement: "We've just had a baby!" He was father of four grown children and my first thought was a new grandchild had been born. "We just watched it wobble out of the nest into the sun." I'd never seen Dick more jubilant. The drama of witnessing a baby condor on a sunny ledge in the backcountry kept mounting as Dick described the vigil he'd kept on the nest site for over a year. Before he finished talking (we were rooted on the sidewalk for 40 minutes), he agreed to write his Condor Journal.

We were both elated. It would be the story of Dick's personal observations of the condor, beginning back in the early 60s and culminating with the hatching of the new chick. He would describe his weekly expeditions deep into the backcountry—a terrain he'd roamed for 20 years and knew like the back of his hand. He would portray his dog, his horse, his *companeros,* as they made camp, scaled cliffs, hiked canyons, bucked dense chaparral while lugging food, water, telescopes and cameras, and sitting on camouflaged promontories for days at a time.

Why would a man put himself through such ordeals for the sake of observing relics from the Pleistocene Age, apparently doomed and of no use to modern man? Dick put it this way: "Think of the condor as a miner's canary." He let this image sink in. The miner carries a canary to test the air. If the canary dies, the miner is in danger. Dick saw the condor as America's environmental canary.

Beyond that, he was an incorrigible romantic who saw the flight of that enormous bird as awesome. The rush of its whistling wings struck passion in his heart. Dick's untimely death prevented him from completing the book we planned. Nevertheless, his journal entries, photos and sketches survived and were expertly assembled and edited by his wife, Olive.

What follows are selected entries over a fourteen-year period. His entries are often cursory and scarcely give the full measure of his experience as he might have written them for a book. You must read between the lines to understand what it was to be a condor-watcher, watching condors wheeling in the sky, chasing off hawks, ravens and eagles—and other days simply staring at the empty heavens.

—NY

1964

Sunday, June 28

My son, Joel, and I arrived at Reyes Peak in mid-morning. This mountain is part of a range lying some 20 miles due west of the Sespe Condor Sanctuary and is directly in the flight line of the birds we had often seen in the Santa Barbara backcountry.

Waldo Abbott of the Museum of Natural History told us he had seen the same condor every day for five days at exactly 1215 hours during the previous week. We found the bird to be 30 minutes late, for he came over, flying west, at 1246. He came close enough to allow for several photographs and showed great curiosity at our presence. He made two low circles above us before resuming his westerly flight.

We were struck by the bird's "old" appearance. He appeared worn and tattered. Several feathers were missing and the white markings were not clean and bright.

* * *

Monday, August 24-29

Joel and I watched for condors on Reyes Peak for five days. We arrived at Reyes Peak road end late Monday afternoon and hiked to the summit. View showed heavy smoke from a fire in the Sespe Wild Area, about 25 miles east in the Coast Range. Sky was brilliant blue with stratus cloud formations and sunspots showing a rainbow effect—possibly caused by smoke in air. The fire had started Sunday in a remote part of the Wild Area behind Fillmore and was nine miles from the condor roosting area in Hopper Canyon.

We planned to watch and record the flight of the birds over the Sierra Madre Mountains and to note the danger to the birds by deer hunters who frequent the ridge on a passable road built by the Standard Oil Company many years ago during a search for oil on Reyes Peak.

Tuesday

No condors today. Watched an eagle being chased by a Cooper's hawk. Later, two Cooper's hawks put on a flying show. They would fly high in the air, then dive at each other. Then they caught a thermal and disappeared high in the sky.

Wednesday

Up at 0630 and on top of peak by 1000. Meant to get to top earlier, but were distracted by a covey of quail and we also stopped to pick raspberries. We strung a tarp between two rocks. Nearly all day in this spot—scanning a full sweep. Signs of smoke boiling up near lookout on Topatopa Mountain. Down at 1900 hours; no sign of condors today.

Thursday

Walked down the face of the mountain on the Sespe side. Beautiful rock and meadow formations, but no sign of life anywhere. Toilet paper flying from bushes, branches and rocks halfway down. Up at saddle by 1130. A young, full-colored but small condor suddenly zoomed over. He caught me by surprise and I ran for my camera but was so excited I had to lie on the ground to get a steady shot. The bird circled once, quite close, then flew over the canyon to the west, dropped his legs and made a landing in the shade where we lost sight of him. Joel and I kept our eyes on the spot where he might have landed, then ran a mile up the road and climbed down as far as we dared. No sign of a feeding or perching bird. We were two hours getting back to our post.

No activity, except two small hawks halfway up Reyes Peak who took turns trying to knock each other off a treetop perch. One would fly high, then drop directly down toward the perched bird who would hold until the very moment of impact, then leap out, away and up. The other bird then took the perch and the daring show continued.

1600 hours. Scanned the sky to the west and saw a black spot moving directly toward us—getting larger. I asked Joel to check with the spotting scope. At this instant he shouted, "Hold it, look overhead!" as a condor flew low over the rock outcrop where we sat. This bird looked older than the one we saw earlier, the primaries not in as good shape and the underwings not as white. He dropped down into the canyon, wings slightly retracted and legs extended as though to find a perch. I ran down the hill, cautioning Joel to keep his eye on the distant bird.

The condor was circling tightly in the trees followed by a golden eagle who didn't get too close. I could not see clearly enough to get a picture.

Within ten minutes, the second condor passed over, accompanied by golden eagles who closed in on him occasionally. A small hawk—an accipiter—dived and nearly hit him, but we watched the

15

majestic condor turn over on his back and roll off to avoid the hawk's rush. This condor came down so close that he was too big an image for the 800 mm lens. I could only get his head and part of one shoulder in the viewfinder. (This, we determined later, would be about 110 feet.) · He circled about 15 times; clockwise first—6 times, then after soaring to Reyes Peak, counterclockwise. He stayed close as I flopped and kicked on my back on the side of the hill. Both condors soared in sight until 1710 hours.

Total for the day—three in all—two strong whole birds and one slightly tattered. All adults, these were the first we've seen since we arrived Monday eve.

Friday
Walked up to the lower rocks and watched several groups of hunters moving about. One or two shots had been fired at a pair of golden eagles earlier, we saw one bird duck and veer off twice when we heard shots. Left at 1630 and drove to Toad Springs and camped.

Saturday
In the morning we went to the top of Cerro Noroeste Mountain and on the way, we saw a condor flying to the west. As we watched, it joined nine other condors flying along the edges of Blue Ridge which goes down from Brush Peak. As we stopped to check with binoculars to see if they were all in full plumage—they seemed to be—there were three more birds circling the top of Brush Peak. These did not follow the ten who went down toward the west. We made a quick decision to follow these ten. A road, headed for Highway 399, was right along their route, and we kept one or two of them in sight for several miles before they all scattered out over the cattle lands east of the Elkhorn.

* * *

(Several attempts were made during the fall of 1964 to photograph condors feeding. Carcasses were placed in safe areas and Dick spent many hours hidden in makeshift blinds, but while condors occasionally flew over the bait, and sometimes circled, none came down. Crows and ravens often betrayed his presence by flying directly in front of the blind and screaming at him, effectively warning all other birds away.)

Wednesday, November 25-29

At Zaca Ladera Ranch we placed two dead heifers on a potrero. This looked like a better place than Reyes Peak. The ranch is closed to the public. Joel and I sighted two birds flying high above the second peak west of Zaca. They landed in a dead pine near the top of the peak. They were still there when we left the blind just before dark.

Thursday

Thanksgiving Day, returned with daughters, Maren and Judy. Condors flew from over the ridge and roosted in the same tree where they had been the night before. They did not respond to the bait. Only two birds in the air at any time, but thought I could see three on the roosting tree.

(*Daughter Maren's note:* Camped a half mile from carcasses because of the smell. Couldn't sleep because of maggots, the sound of them chewing was so loud.)

Saturday

One of the heifers had lost its tail to a coyote. At 0925, I saw two birds come over the ridge to settle on the roost. I watched them stretch and air their wings in the morning sun until 0950. I moved up the mountain to see if I could get closer to the birds on the roost. As I was walking up a canyon, I saw a juvenile condor fly down the ridge to my left. His head was not orange and there was little white under his wings. The other birds I had seen that morning were beautifully marked with well defined white wing patterns and strong yellow-orange head color.

At 1200, I was even with the roost tree but about an eighth of a mile to the west. The birds had flown. I found their roosting trees well used. Saw no more birds by the time I left.

Sunday

I crawled into my blind and waited. No birds appeared until 1400. Two adults flew to the roost peak where they were joined by a juvenile. Obviously this is a family group. I watched the three birds soar in ever-rising circles; they rose until almost out of sight, then descended and drifted out over Foxen Canyon.

Spent a great part of the following week watching from a blind on the potrero. I saw birds—condors and golden eagles—every day. They never came down to the bait.

* * *

Sunday, December 11

Joel and I went to the top of Zaca Peak, walked the trail out to the slope where we had seen condors in a dead pine. We found no feathers or sign of droppings. Near the tree, however, we found the remains of a female deer, picked nearly clean. After finding this, we gave up the watch over the baited potrero.

1965

Sunday, January 17

Matilija Canyon, 1535 hours, heavy wind, gusts up to 50 mph on mountain top, sky clear. Condor coming over ridge to north, soaring exceptionally fast. With 20-power binoculars could see white and yellow-orange clearly because of low sun lighting underside. Assuming the bird's height to be only 5280 feet above observer, the distance covered, three miles and the time it took the bird to cross the visible sky was 2½ minutes, then the speed would be about 100 mph.

To me, the important point of this observation was the direction and speed of flight. The bird was independent of any thermal. It was not merely hunting, for it was flying across canyons where one seldom observes them at a lower height. The bird was moving contrary to surface winds and at an extremely high elevation and speed.

* * *

Saturday, March 6-7

Trip with Bob Easton to Piru area. While walking along the top of the Santa Felicia Dam, we saw a condor soaring high above us. This sighting gave us hope of seeing more birds, so we drove along a narrow road following the creek above the lake. Saw three more condors in the air.

About 1410, we started back toward Piru. Near the edge of the town, saw two condors soaring above a ridge. We stopped and watched the two birds, then saw a young bird drop down the canyon toward us. It came close enough so we could see that the head was dark . . . no white under the wings.

While I was trying to put the camera, lens, extender and a tripod together, Bob used 20-power binoculars. He was watching three, not two birds and now one was dropping down to a dead animal where several more condors were feeding. I thought he was joking. I took the binoculars and saw seven condors in all, fighting for position on a dead cow. We watched for a few minutes, then realized we should find out who could give us permission to get on the property.

Drove back to the Black Ranch house where we were given permission. We returned to the canyon. By this time it was raining and we could see the birds had left the carcass. Tomorrow would have to do.

The two King brothers agreed that the number of condors seen around dead animals on the ranch had diminished from around 30 or more in the 1930s to about 9 today.

Sunday

Bob and I returned. At 0700 we began to climb the steep hill. It was higher and farther back than we had thought. We found a bush in the right place and dug a hollow under it . . . in front and around it we laid branches of chamise. A tarp on the ground and one overhead completely covered with twigs—made what we thought would be an adequate cover. In fact, we were so well concealed it was going to be hard to take a photograph.

It hadn't occurred to us that the big problem would be the critical inspection of our hideaway by crows! At 0830 a flock of fifteen or more crows came in sight, hovered over the carcass, then began to caw and talk in an excited manner.

One crow broke away from the flock and flew directly toward our blind, about 200 feet away. It hovered in front of the small opening

19

and made a variety of low sounds, not unlike a man talking to himself. Another crow came over, then another. They all babbled and flew up and down around our blind.

Two vultures came on the scene. They acted as though the talking of the crows and the loud caws they made served as a warning. Obviously we were not passing "inspection."

A heavy rush of air right over our blind almost shook loose some of our branches. A condor, an adult, with white well-marked on the underside of its wings, went soaring toward the bait. It was called to and rushed by the crows hovering nearby. Through one corner of the blind I saw another condor directly overhead. It did not come down, but I was able to observe the bird's head moving back and forth as though trying to see into our hiding place.

The birds all left . . . only occasionally did the crows come back. They were cautious. One hovered in front of the peephole for a moment or two. We felt he had looked us right in the eyes!

After two and a half hours of sitting in a cramped position without uttering a word, Bob and I got out to stretch . . . decided to climb the hill at the back so we could look into Hopper Canyon. We saw a condor—not too high and moving slowly.

I dropped to the ground and flapped my arms and legs. The bird turned and dropped lower. It circled three times before resuming its flight.

As we neared the crest, two more condors came over quite high, followed by another. I would judge their height to be more than 8000 feet and climbing fast.

On the top at 1145. Several birds were riding a thermal just above the ridge. Almost at a signal, all began to move north and were joined by others above Dominguez Canyon, all circled and rose. We counted seven. None of them had come back from the southeast. This would make nine or ten in the air at one time in the Piru area.

1400 hours. Bob in the blind and I in a tight little wash filled with vegetation. I had wrapped myself in chilicothe vines and was deep in the brush, lying on my back. A crow came over to within a few feet of my head. It called another and the two looked me over. I was so sure I would not be spotted, and yet, here were the crows. They would not go near the carcass.

We gave up at 1530 hours.

* * *

20

Sunday, June 20-24

Left Santa Barbara with Bob, Ginger Easton and the two Easton horses at 1600. Saw condor over hill west of road above Cachuma Saddle at 1730. In dark on way up, found a small "glow" bug—a larva—put it in film box to have identified.

Monday

Up the grade toward Hurricane Deck. Coming down to Happy Hunting Ground found creek dry. Went on to crossing where water was good. Small dragonfly nymphs—took pix. A USFS patrolman came by asking if we had seen condors. He was gathering information for the Service.

Tuesday

I awoke and climbed to top of hill overlooking the Sisquoc River. Took pictures of sunrise over the valley. After breakfast we went up the South Fork past the narrows—huge potholes—big rock formation, stream orchids, lots of fish. Later Bob, Ginger and I went up White Ledge Creek to Sulphur Pool. Water not too hot, but warm enough to be comfortable. We swam. After we got back, caught some bigger fish for a total of 17. I cleaned them and Bob fried them in bacon fat . . . wonderful!

Wednesday

Made a dry camp a quarter mile up from Skunk Camp. Then we hiked up river trail to the Rattlesnake and swam in the pools. I rode to the top, saw two condors and a golden eagle flying above the sanctuary at 1800. Ginger had seen them all along.

Thursday

Started observing on hill above sanctuary. A bird in top trees above falls, can't identify. Bob and I climbed a ridge above canyon back of Skunk Camp. Up a rocky wash—almost straight up for the first 150 feet with only tiny potholes for hand and footholds. Getting the camera gear up was hazardous, we slipped and slid several times. Then bucked brush to go west far enough to see the falls. From this vantage could see a pool behind the overhanging dropoff. As for the falls, they are varied enough to keep one's attention for hours. The play of light in the morning, the sparkle of sun on the dramatic fall of water, as the wind in the canyon whips the stream first one way and then another. This first fall descends free for at least 250 to 350 feet to

21

a ledge of mossy rock that splits it into a wide ribbon of water spilling down into the trees and out of sight.

After coming down we made time for swimming in a small deep pool below Skunk Camp. Washed clothes, then came up for supper which Bob so nicely fixed. I was too tired from bucking brush to be of help. Walked downstream and viewed falls from a lower angle in the late sun.

Saw several ant lion holes and dug one out to show Ginger. Boiled some mugwort leaves for a poultice on my poison oak "possibles" in the scratches I got pushing through the dry brush. Also picked a small black pod, with thistle-like silver-white tips. (Note: Identified by Clif Smith of Museum of Natural History as *Collomia grandiflora*— Phlox family.)

* * *

Sunday, October 17

First Annual Condor Survey. Assigned station on Mission Pine trail with Swede Hansen, USFS.

1122, possible condor 8 to 10 miles WNW from observation point flying north over McPherson Pk.

1255, condor stayed above about 9 minutes. Came from SE, circled 5 times. Adult bird, full plumage, good condition. Not too large. Came down to 150 ft.

1340, condor circling about 2 miles NW above skyline over Sweetwater Canyon. In sight for about a minute.

Sedges growing in creek, cattails in some places. Asters along trail. Large stands of dry tocalote above South Fork. Large cherry bushes in full fruit, taste good. Bear tracks up into bushes, large scat full of berry seeds.

Large quail, about 20 at gate west of station. Not afraid. Heard Chaparral wren, jays above South Fork, pair of ravens in Falls Canyon at noon. Badger holes in trail. Pool filled with trout and some chubs. Sharp water grass, 6 ft. high. Few piñon nuts around on top this year.

1966

Wednesday, April 13

Interview with William Edwards, age 78:

"I was about 14, the year must have been 1902. Billy Gallagher, Arthur Ogilvy and I went up Cold Spring Creek and found a condor egg in a ledge of rock beside the falls. We saw the two birds and they weren't happy that we were trying to climb up to their nest. Billy, I think, was the one who got up to the place where we thought we would look. The condors were not visible when we first started up. They came out of the rock just above us and you can imagine how surprised we were when we saw their wingspread. These were the only condors I ever saw on this side of the mountain. Well, Billy got up there. A face of the rock had moved out leaving a deep depression . . . It was behind this that the egg was lying. There was no actual nest. They don't make a nest, you know. I took off my pants and threw them up to Billy. He crawled down and put the egg in a leg of my pants after he had tied a knot in it. He lowered the egg down and we rushed back to town.

"We went straight to Dr. Yates, who ran the Natural History Museum downtown in an adobe building. Dr. Yates offered to blow the egg for us. He found it contained a partially formed bird and cut a small circle of the shell from one end and with forceps removed the body. He then put the egg back together and gave it to us. We knew it was useless each to have a third share in a condor egg, so we advertised in a local newspaper. We sold it to a man from San Luis Obispo for $40."

* * *

23

Wednesday, August 10

0500, had trouble loading Josephine, my new horse, in trailer. This made me late for the trip to Pleito Creek Indian cave painting area. Made a jeep trip with Doug Hayden down a creek bed from Neason Ridge. Saw old homesteads and cave paintings. Even though this hot valley canyon is virtually impossible to get to, there are many tracks of people at caves.

Back before 1550 and climbed to Pinos in truck. Several people watching condors at radar station. Saw a condor light on a limb just below me and got some pix. Birds are using the mountain as base of operations. There have been 10 birds around for several days. They come close overhead and watch people.

Counted 21 condors in air at one time over Sawmill Mountain.

* * *

Saturday, August 20-21

Sawmill Mt. with Jim Mills. Hunter at end of ridge sitting in rocks. Cooper's hawk flying past ducked and dipped. Sound of gunshot. Second dip, second shot heard. Third shot and the bird tumbled from the air.

Hunter's companion came by. I went with him to talk to his friend. Both aware of the $1,000 fine for shooting a condor. Neither could identify two condors overhead, thought they were eagles. 1015, adult condor soared by, out over the valley. When it passed the hunters, it dipped and fluttered. Then I heard a shot. The bird straightened, circled and resumed flight. 1245 through the afternoon, condors in all directions—low and high.

1415. Two juvenile condors soaring to north of Sawmill. Birds dropped into canyon between Sawmill and Mt. Pinos. I heard a shot. One juvenile flew up out of canyon. This was the last time we saw two juveniles. Total seen at one time—six adults and two juveniles.

Sunday

1215. Six condors circling for ten minutes. During this time the birds engaged in some interesting actions. One would lower its legs, pull in its wings and drop down to a bird below. Bird thus attacked would slip off to side and the aggressor would repeat the action. I was struck by the similarity to children trying to force one child to be the first to look at something new or dangerous.

Left the blind at 1620 and checked the canyon below. There were seven condors, one in black stage, roosting in live and dead Jeffrey pines and Big Cone Spruce. When I tried to get close they all rose and moved to the north slope. When I followed, they moved again. As I crossed the saddle trail at 1820, I saw them still in trees on the ridge all in a line.

* * *

Saturday, September 3

My son-in-law, Rod Soria, and I got to Mt. Pinos-Sawmill Mt. area by 1500 hours. Condors in air. A couple from Glendale said they saw eight condors in air west of Sawmill. We went out on a granite ledge and sat—watched birds. 1700, in tree and near a spring we saw two and three birds at a time drinking, others perching. One flew and I made a rabbit noise that brought it right over. It was an adult. Flew west and then back, this time close.

Each condor would dip its head into the shallow water, throw its head back, then straighten up, stretch its wings, repeat the process, then flap up on a rock above falls and spread its wings to dry. At least eight birds, mixed young and adults. I was so intent on watching them bathe I did not keep track of ages. There were at least two with dark heads and white underwings. One of them appeared all black.

While some were in the pool others were flying overhead, moving to and from the nearby trees. This so intrigued me I set up a blind not far from the pool on Sunday. From 1100 to 1700, I saw only three condors fly over. None showed interest in the water and continued on without even turning their heads.

1967

Monday, April 17-22

Five-day pack trip to West Big Pine and Mission Pine Basin with John Borneman, Audubon Condor Naturalist, and Fred Sibley, U.S. Fish and Wildlife Biologist. Easton's Rusty as packhorse.

Tuesday

Awoke to overcast, light rain and snow. Waited until 1500 for weather to clear, then loaded packs on trusty Rusty and on up to Big Pine. Snow 2 ft. deep at top. On way to West Big Pine we came to a fallen tree and it took several attempts to lead Rusty through deeper side hill snow to get past—frightening. Realized we were in for a bad night. Fred went on ahead to open lookout. Temperature dropping fast, nerve-wracking wind. Could hardly bring myself to climb last stretch of snow-choked road. John struggling on behind, old knee injury really bothering him in heavy going.

Horse sweating. Decided to take him inside shack below lookout. Fred and I had hell of a time getting him through door, but afraid to leave him without drying off. We rubbed him down, then rigged a tarp at side of shack so we could move him out for night. Temperature down to 20°, snowing now.

Wednesday

Abandoned plan to visit Mission Pine Basin, loaded Rusty and started back down. At least 4″ of snow. Cold but excitingly beautiful. Spent rest of day at Bluff Camp. Snow several feet deep, rain and snow all day.

Thursday

20° at 0600. Took Grapevine Trail to Santa Cruz Guard Station. Tied Rusty to a sapling near our camp. He heard horses at the station and joined them, sapling and all.

Friday

Wet and rainy. Moved into stable and spent most of day building fireplace and hunting firewood by creek. Slept warm and dry that night with the mice.

Saturday

Scotty Beaton, the Forest Service packer, offered to take our pack bags and loaned us a saddle so John could ride Rusty. John having

26

difficulty walking. Water at the crossing up to our hips, running swift. Trail covered with wildflowers. Took old trail from Nineteen Oaks, Scotty on ahead, mules and horses going every which way. We ran and laughed all the way to Oso Camp. Swam horses across river. My dog, Sally, had hard time in the fast water and Fred had to help her.

* * *

Tuesday, October 17-18

Annual Condor Survey. Assigned to observation station at Sand Springs Ridge w/Will Griffen, USFS. Three condors at 1046, 2 miles to SE. 1103, two birds moved to Santa Barbara Potrero, in sight sitting on poles along ridge.

Second day. 1515, two adult condors between Big Pine Mt. and Judell Ridge. Circled twice, then down into Logan Canyon.

* * *

Wednesday, November 29

To Zaca Ladera Ranch w/Ray Strong. At 1250, we were at Solvang turnoff. Saw two large birds over the San Lucas Ranch. They began to rise. Stopped and got out the long lens and by the time the camera was ready, they were almost a thousand feet up, rising in a thermal, slowly circling. High above them we saw a pair of immature golden eagles—touches of white under wings, white rump spots.

As we watched, a car stopped on the side of the road. Driver sat watching birds. He thought we were falconers. He had been watching the birds in air and assumed we had let the birds out. His interest was sailplaning and said he was fascinated by soaring birds.

* * *

Saturday, December 23

Audubon Christmas Bird Count w/Brad Schram and Cameron Aanerud. Walked from Juan Fustero Camp to ridge at edge of Sespe Condor Sanctuary. First bird at 1040. Got condor to come over by calling. Saw condor on way to potholes, more when we got there. Total of five for day.

Went down Agua Blanca to Piru Creek—waded through narrows—*cold!* On way back at dusk we saw a poorwill. First one on any bird count.

27

1968

Sunday, February 4-9

With Dennis Cogan to Sisquoc River with three horses, Josephine, Rusty, and Nikka as pack horse. Left Oso Camp and trucked horses in 19 miles, and on trail to Little Pine by 0930. Beautiful day, snow on slopes. Reached Bluff Camp at 1730, overcast and turning cold by dark. Supper in cabin—nice hot fire.

Monday

Cold and windy. From West Big Pine we saw birds in snow on Big Pine Mt.—Golden eagles, ravens, Clark's nutcrackers, Ruby Crowned Kinglet, Stellar' jays.

Bear tracks in snow on trail all the way down to Lower Bear Camp. Camp was a shambles. Only one of three stoves still standing—all others and wooden sign broken by bears. Saw cub tracks farther on—looked like child's footprints. Dug lily bulbs for Museum and Botanic Garden. Clear and cold. Sally slept between us.

Tuesday

At Rattlesnake, just as we scaled a shale ridge, lead rope for pack horse got around and under Josephine's tail. The fun began—we had made the mistake of tying on a pan from breakfast. It banged noisily. That plus the rope around her tail caused Josephine to start down the steep trail with a go-for-broke rush, dragging Nikka, the pack horse. Ahead, Rusty heard the commotion and bucked, Dennis flew off into a fine specimen of *Prunus ilicifolia*. Rusty ran down as far as the river. Josephine, with me still on and Nikka right behind, came on down to the big switchback—a 30 ft. drop. I was at the point of departure from this world and yelled out "Here we go" not having any other sensible thought in my head. Josephine, sweet girl that she is, slid to a halt, forelegs dangling over the edge. Luckily, I had thrown the lead rope free and Nikka skidded to a halt. Dennis was getting up out of the cherry bush. We got to the bottom and shook a few minutes—Dennis, horses and me.

South Fork station. Put horses out. Dennis found an arrowhead almost immediately. Signs of old digs along Sweetwater Trail. Dennis found a mother rock of jasper and beside it, a point of same. Old camp below, lots of juniper in meadow, one stalk of sweet corn growing on river bottom. Lots of quail, deer and coyote tracks around.

Wednesday

1030 over Sisquoc. One condor circling to left of Forrester's Leap. Two Golden eagles, one an immature. Watched condor for ten minutes.

Past Sycamore Camp. Old rock fireplace, metal grown into trees, pile of old horseshoes, mule shoes too, pair of broken buggy wheels. Dug by river and found square whiskey bottle, old beer bottles, vaseline jar—buried them again.

Friday

As we climbed out of a steep canyon, Dennis called out that he heard glass break. I dismounted and went back to check lantern in pack. As Dennis went around me on trail, Nikka leaned toward me and the lantern fell with a crash! Josephine lit out like a bomb, and Nikka right behind her, leaving me standing on the trail hollering "Head them off!" but Dennis was off on another mad ride. Horses finally stopped on a mesa and started to feed—Dennis said, "Hell, when you said head 'em off I was praying just to stay on."

29

After supper back at schoolhouse we heard a big sigh. Turned the lantern and saw Nikka lie down and close her eyes. Poor girl has been sleeping standing up like other horses for days and days.

* * *

Thursday, November 21

Let horses rest today, walked to Pine Corral Potrero. Marnie sketched while I photographed rocks. 1215, saw two adult condors to east—about 4 miles, but could see their orange-yellow heads with glasses. They dropped down toward Cuyama.

Saw several golden eagles fly into canyon that leads to Lion Canyon. We followed into nearly impassable places—damp and mossy, deep pools in rocks. Finally into a tight canyon with vertical walls of solid rock with lots of caves. Some bird nests—ravens, hawks. Down into a slit as narrow as 4 ft.—jumped through puddles—ended up looking straight down into Lion Canyon—40 ft. drop.

1969

Tuesday, April 1-4

South Fork of Sisquoc River with Dean Carrier, USFS Biologist. On trail by 0830. About three miles out on Sweetwater Trail an adult condor soared up from Forrester's Leap Canyon, heading north. Fog has lifted—light east wind, some haze in air. Bird out of sight at 0941. Spotted two condors at 0943 on ridge north of Pine Corral Potrero.

Wednesday

Surprised a rattlesnake—11 buttons. Left it. Walked to top of rocks to see if Carrier could get over by rope to check out holes below that showed whitewash (bird excrement). One was reachable. It contained what appeared to be owl droppings. The highest one was out of reach. At 1513, while on slope, we sighted an adult condor flying due south from Pine Corral Potrero. It turned over the Sisquoc River and flew west. We raced for the top of the hill and watched it disappear over the eastern end of the Hurricane Deck. Clouds were beginning to look threatening. Raced back and got to South Fork as rain began falling.

Thursday

Arrived Blue Falls at 1340. Place is fabulous. Canyon below is wonderful—air filled with light mist from falls. Climbed lower side of falls steeply to top. Found two good bathing pools. Carrier thought there might be too much water running now but they would be excellent for condors when water slows down. One good feather on ground below a rock outcrop. It measures exactly 15 inches long and the quill is 1-15/16 inches to the ridge. Good condition with only a few rodent teeth marks on the quill and a small portion of the vane missing.

Friday

Packed up, cleaned cabin. Made river crossing and checked ledges across river. One hole closest to South Fork looks good. It shows considerable whitewash. I saw a large bird—possibly with a yellow-orange head, sitting on a rock ledge down river. By the time we got out the spotting scope, it was gone. Back on trail—we spotted two adult condors headed down Forrester's Leap Canyon. At 1003, they were out of sight behind hills. Sky clear and little breeze, temperature in 50s. At 1016, two adult condors about two miles away—in sight until 1021. Carrier believes second sighting to be the same birds.

* * *

31

Wednesday, October 15-20

Annual Condor Survey. Ray Dalen, USFS, and I went to top of mountain on Sierra Madre Ridge, found USFS pickup, trailer, horse and mule waiting. Packed up and headed for Sweetwater Trail.

Thursday

Climbed rock outcrop west of trail on meadow above South Fork. Had good view of bluffs Carrier and I had checked last year. All day and only eagles. Then sighted a pair of condors at 1550 headed down ridge west of Sweetwater. Watched them land in trees above Blue Falls junction.

Saturday

Saw a dead cow below spring. Looked like it had fallen from ledge above—quite old, meat gone, but fresh bear tracks and droppings around. More bear tracks on way back to car.

Monday

End of ridge west of station. Saw what appeared to be seven condors below, circling close as though feeding.

ONE SMALL WING FEATHER

ONE COVERLET

ONE COVERLET

ALL FOUND ON LEDGE ABOVE FALLS— (SISQUOC)

1971

Tuesday, July 13-15

South Fork of Sisquoc River with Dean Carrier and Monty Montagne, USFS Biologist. Climbed to high rocks SW of the South Fork where I found a condor's covert feather.

Wednesday

Long walk to Blue Falls—river rough to hike. Dean and Monty climbed side of falls and along cliffs upstream until I sighted them in on whitewash near top. Dean couldn't find a way to hang over the edge to look. There was only old whitewash flaking off.

Thursday

Saddled horses and rode to top of Mission Pine Falls Trail where Dean checked old nest site. No new whitewash. Back down to Falls Canyon junction. Swam for half hour then took Monty up opposite hill to see falls flowing. Long hike. Beautiful falls. Lots of five-fingered maidenhair, other ferns. Moist air, deep pool—at least 20 ft. Carrier climbed to first ledge where falls break, found four small body feathers—fresh. No activity in air all day. Collected plants all the way down to Sisquoc for Clif Smith at the Museum of Natural History. Bathed—saddled up and back to cabin by 1830. HOT. Bathed again. Dean cooked burritos in camp . . . five each. Priscilla, my young hound, ate four. She's really tired tonight.

1972

Monday, April 24-26

To South Fork of Sisquoc with Dean, Monty. Horses saddled and waiting at Santa Barbara Potrero windmill. Packed our gear on FS mules, went down to Heath Camp. Saw fresh bear tracks on Judell Trail. Dumped our pack gear in rocks at camp below junction, then rode up—pulling mules—all the way to the falls on upper Sisquoc. Water is lower than in other years.

Tuesday

Down to Falls Canyon. Dean and I checked for condor sign. Saw a juvenile at 0927—in sight soaring due north for three minutes. Spent several hours in canyon, saw fresh whitewash on face of falls. Dean climbed to top and had tough time getting back down.

Wednesday

Walked up hill on south side of Sisquoc and checked nest site on top, then all the way to edge of White Ledge. Lots of old trail markers—rocks—along ledge.

Saturday

Followed jeep trail to south of Pine Canyon, saw a condor circling over Madulce lookout. 1530, two condors circling Madulce Ridge in a mating display or perhaps just play.

* * *

1973

In 1973, observations concentrated in an area where condors were suspected to be nesting. Many experts believe there are two distinct condor populations—one nesting in or near the Sespe Condor Sanctuary and foraging as far north as the Sierra foothills in Tulare County, while the other nests and ranges from the San Rafael Wilderness along the Pacific Coast mountains to San Jose in Santa Clara County. This Coast Range population and the suspected nesting site were the focus of observations from 1973 until 1977.

Dick Smith joined Forest Service personnel in regular visits to determine if condors were nesting in a remote area where juvenile birds had been observed recently. As a research associate of the Museum of Natural History, he and staff members represented the Museum in this joint Coast Range Condor Survey. By 1976, the observations were being made monthly, weather permitting.

To protect this sensitive area from intrusion, the following journal entries have been deliberately altered, as Dick insisted. Each trip involved a drive of several hours from Santa Barbara to a base camp where horses were unloaded, packed with cameras, telescopes and food. From there it was steep trail and rough going to the observation site.

Thursday, January 4-6. To Monolith Ridge w/Jerry Berry, USFS.

We were searching through wind caves for possible Indian paintings and artifacts. Then we crossed over the top and followed a cleft down a sandstone monolith. There, almost within reach, sat a young black-headed condor! Its ruff extended in the wind. The bird was less than 250 feet away. I went out on a steep sloping rock to get a better look and a picture. Below we saw whitewash on top of a ledge. We walked down to it, watching the bird as we went. It followed us with its head until we reached the back side of the rock. The youngster expressed great interest in his human visitors . . . very curious as we worked our way down toward his pinnacle roost. He was perched just under the peak where a hole went all the way through. He seemed very curious about the dog, Priscilla, and stretched his head and neck around each time she broke a twig pushing through the brush. As we made our way below the pinnacle rock, the bird flew. We saw him a moment later and he circled low, looking us over. He then headed east to another group of rocks, flapping a few times to get there. He landed and promptly spread his wings with the sun on his back. Kept his wings flexed and arched forward for almost five minutes. Then he flew and circled the area, coming close each time I waved and called. Several whitewash areas marked top of ledge below the main rock, but the nest appears more likely in the upper half of the monolith. Jerry found a flight feather about 18 inches long.

We sighted an adult condor at 1515, in the air looking us over. As we watched, the young bird flew up from somewhere below and rose to meet the adult. Lost sight of them as we moved down from our brush-bound position to a whitewashed Big Cone Spruce snag. Feathers all over ground and whitewash scattered on underbrush. Leaves also showed burns from older excrement. Through binoculars we saw whitewashed tree snags in a canyon to west.

Friday

Walked up river to the west, past flats with oaks, then climbed to a second flat and back below monolith. We followed an amazing frozen stream stopped by a quick freeze . . . icicles everywhere. Climbed hard, smooth, steep rockfaces for several hundred feet to reach top of ridge. Crawled over the edge of ridge to base of two trees covered with whitewash.

1515, after coming up from narrows we sat on rock promontory above roost trees . . . suddenly a heavy sound like some kind of machinery directly overhead. We looked up . . . soaring from behind us along the ridge were two adult condors 50 feet above. The sound of their whistling wings was accompanied by an undertone vibration. The sound became a hissing whistle as they soared on to the east. No sign of the young condor.

Saturday

1015, Jerry spotted young bird on east roost tree. He occasionally stretches his wings in the sun. Appears to have been left alone for the night. Then an adult flew over at 500 ft. The moment it passed over the roost tree, the young bird took off. Immediately a second condor was in sight. All three flying close together. One adult landed on the monolith where we had seen the young one on the first day. The others circled the rock for three minutes . . . then the seated adult was airborne and all soared in high and low circles as though giving the youngster a flying lesson. At times he had to flap his wings to keep up. Then he landed on the monolith as the parents circled out of sight below horizon at 1215.

* * *

Friday, July 27. Check of Monolith Ridge site w/Dean.

Found a fresh body feather and a primary under roost tree west of site. This is a Big Cone Spruce approximately 80 ft. tall. Fresh whitewash on brush under tree, roost branches also white.

Whitewash showed at back of hole in monolith but Carrier felt it was too shallow to be a nest. Looked through binoculars at lower hole and observed young plants growing in the bottom. Back and sides showed whitewash. Roost tree below has fresh whitewash.

On way back up Dean found a flight or secondary feather beneath one ledge. Observed another hole with extensive whitewash but found no feathers or eggshell below. Photos from January trip show no whitewash then.

(*Ed. note:* Visit in Fall 1977 shows this shallow hole to have been a nest cave. Extensively whitewashed interior still visible, fragments of eggshell found, samples of shell and nest floor material taken for analysis.)

1974

Monday, April 8. Check of Monolith Ridge site w/Monty.

Big Cone Spruce to west shows no recent sign of roosting. Watched all day but no condors.

Overcast, snow in air. Sun breaking through occasionally, temperature in mid 40s. Found only old whitewash on farthest west group of trees. Moved to trees on far east of pinnacle and found a fresh left primary that measures 26¼ inches long, in excellent condition. No rodent gnawing.

A hole at base of a reef opposite had been filled with oak duff and made into a bed by a bear. We had observed a large bright brown bear on a steep meadow about a mile away as we went out to the rocks in the morning.

Moved directly under hole observed in 1973 and saw extensive whitewash at back. This hole is about 25 ft. above ground on steeply declining reef of light sandstone. Found a right primary 26¼" long, sun faded, cracked quill with extensive loss of feather material from rodent gnawing.

* * *

Sunday, July 7—With Harley Greiman, USFS, and Carl Koford.

Special trip into the Los Padres National Forest during fire closure. We had three objectives: to collect botanical specimens blooming above 5000 ft. after area is closed, to investigate mountain lion use of area for study in progress by Carl Koford, Museum of Vertebrate Zoology of University of California, and to check condor activity in and near the Sisquoc Sanctuary because of early spring reports of sightings.

Mission Pine Spring by 1600. Collected *Lilium pardalinum,* orchid and mint at spring and creek to north.

Down Falls Canyon trail, we saw whitewash on rocks above falls. Trail overgrown, going back to nature. Collected grasses, some flowers, also hard bush with small purple-red pea flowers all along trail. Mint in Falls Creek and an interesting fern.

Manzanita doesn't appear to have burls, but they are there—small and covered. Low plants all along trails. *Collomia* on potreros under pines. Indian hemp in open washes of basin. Creek bed thick with bur clover. Recent bear scat and tracks all along trail.

Carl described lion tracks and how to distinguish them from other large animals. Showed how lion makes scratch marks. Both feet together in duff—pine or oak leaves, leaving a pile at end of 10 or 12 inch scratch.

Saw bear tracks over our earlier ones on way back to springs. Carl saw tracks later near camp, but food wasn't touched.

Scrub jays, olive-sided flycatchers, Anna's hummingbirds, Oregon juncos, towhees, red-tailed hawks, a great horned owl and a marsh hawk were about all the birds seen. Lots of mountain quail tracks but no birds.

1975

Thursday, February 27. Check of area observed during 1973 and 1974 w/Monty.

Reached Base Camp at 1000. Moved out and spent an hour looking over Monolith Ridge area where we feel condors may have nested in 1972. No sign of use on rocks and trees.

Farther along, we glassed the Escarpment and checked entire face for signs of whitewash or bird activity. Suddenly, two condors appeared at west end nearly three miles away. They appeared to have come from somewhere on lower cliff face, soaring and moving east, then out of sight. We kept a close watch and saw them reappear above the cliffs, circle and land on a rock outcrop at the base. At 1155 we saw them again above skyline. They caught a thermal, rose up and then dropped away behind Escarpment.

We walked up a firebreak. From here, I observed a large bird sitting on a rock promontory. We glassed the area until 1514 when the bird took off and we saw it was an adult condor. It spiralled up until it gained an altitude of approximately 10,000 ft. and headed away to the north. Birds seem to be showing more than a casual interest in this general area.

* * *

Tuesday, April 1-2. Escarpment area w/Monty.

On way up to Base Camp, Priscilla jumped from the back of truck and injured a hind leg so we had to put her in the cab. We left her in truck at end of road and hiked up to check area of 1973 observations. No sign of birds. Walked several miles through patches of snow to where we could climb out to the west edge of the Escarpment where we had seen birds on roosts in February . . . no whitewash, no feathers.

Hiked downhill to north and thought I saw a large bird disappear to the east. Then as I came up to the northeast, I saw a fully marked condor and a golden eagle appear to the east. I heard Monty blowing a predator call and looked back up the slope. Right above him was another fully marked condor. Quickly I climbed up to Monty as the condors met and began to circle. Then both lowered their wings, raised them again, extended their legs and landed on a ledge just below the top of the cliff—West Roost rock. The birds stood facing each other. They crossed necks, rubbed. One raised its head as the other put its head against its partner's beak. At first it appeared to be courtship or feeding, but Monty decided it might be pair bonding. One was shiny black, the other a dullish brown. One's head was pale orange, the other a red-orange. Both had full white pattern under wings. These two birds circled on the rock, alternately facing each other and standing side by side. At 1442, a third adult appeared and passed around the cliff to the north. One of the pair lifted off with a flap. The other followed, but with one or two clumsy flaps. Three condors circling now at 1455. One landed on a rock outcrop above the first ledge. Others continued circling and then soared off to the north.

As we watched the roosting bird, an immature golden eagle flew directly toward it and swooped down close. The condor flapped and flew off, down and around the rock face with the eagle in close pursuit. At 1518, a condor landed close to the top of cliff, then left with flapping wings at 1518. We couldn't see where it went.

Wednesday

Monty called me to look straight up. A condor soared directly from Monolith Ridge north over Base Camp, then caught a thermal, circled twice and headed for the Escarpment where we had seen bird in late afternoon the day before. Now two condors soared into view from the north and passed above the roosting bird. This one rose, appeared to have jumped up, then landed again and remained perched as the others disappeared back to the north.

41

Conclusion: The conduct of these three birds during our observations in February and April would seem to indicate a family, although there is no pattern difference. There could be a female with an egg to tend who stays near a nest hole rather than forage all day. But this raises a question about the two ranging adults returning to a possible nest. They bear further observation.

* * *

Wednesday, April 16. Observation of Escarpment from firebreak on ridge south of Base Camp w/Monty and Steve Bishop, USFS Biologist

Climbed firebreak until we could look across at face of Escarpment. 0943, condor with white underwings sat on rock to west of our April 1 observation post. It flexed its wings twice, then sat still. At 0955, a second condor appeared above and flew down to the roosting bird who immediately took off. At 0959 only one condor in air. Heavy clouds building up. At 1000, bird has alighted on easternmost ledge of Escarpment. Snow in air. Bird still there.

1220, saw a condor in air over Escarpment as clouds lifted. 1325, condor circling over West Roost rock. As we watched from below, the soaring condor was slowly obscured by lowering snow-laden clouds.

We now have a new question: Where do these two condors roost when not visible from below? They seem to appear and disappear so quickly, as though coming from somewhere near top of Escarpment.

* * *

Thursday, May 1. From the firebreak w/Monty.

1019, saw condor soaring along ridge from Monolith Canyon. Out of sight to west at 1020.

At 1530, condor with adult plumage glided down from Escarpment and circled out to south after soaring directly over us at 300 feet. At 1545, condor returned dropping fast, sailed across face of Escarpment and landed on West Roost rock. The action of lifting wings and extending legs was perfectly visible with 7-power binoculars even though miles away!

As we walked down firebreak, a peregrine falcon slipped directly over us, moving in a quickening wind. Very dark above with bright brown on the breast and obvious sideburns.

* * *

Tuesday, May 13-14. Escarpment w/Monty and Steve.

At 1027 Monty picked up the bright orange-yellow head of a roosting condor about 1000 ft. below. 1042, bird off roost and out of sight below a ledge.

1206, Monty and Steve spotted immature condor, head dark, splotchy white under wings. It landed below. Then an adult made several passes over young bird and both flew up and directly over observation site. 1305, four condors above observation post. Steve and Monty were directly below birds as they circled out and back. In the heavy wind, the condors' wings assumed some well-trimmed positions. Then as birds moved off toward Gavilan Canyon a mile or so north, we could see the immature bird playfully soar close to an adult, flipping its wings in mock battle.

At 1423, immature condor, appearing gawky and slightly clumsy, flew slowly below our post. Its legs were extended as it landed somewhere below a ridge out of sight.

Wednesday

1450, Monty glassed in a dark spot on ledge where we had seen immature bird disappear the afternoon before. Through the scope we recognized the immature condor, feathers shiny black, black head and greyish tinge to heavy ruff covering neck.

Suddenly an adult appeared just below us, young bird moved out of sight as adult follows behind ledge.

Now the adult is above the ledge. It circles slowly as if searching for a thermal. Wings arched. Crosses to west, finds a thermal at edge of ridge and rides it to West Roost rock, then passes over us at 500 ft. Now back along face of Escarpment followed by a turkey vulture. Condor lands on West Roost rock, vulture circles above. The condor scrapes its beak on rock, first one side, then the other.

Two vultures now hover and circle over condor. Its crop is heavily distended. Apparently it has been feeding somewhere below us. Condor leaves roost. At 1628 a second adult from northeast joined first bird. Appears to be missing third right primary, no full crop. 1640, three condors now over West Roost rock. Bird with full crop lands on top of small pine. A second lands on same limb, then third tries, no room. All fly off, try again. Two on limb, other lands on rock. Birds in tree appear to be touching beaks. All show white under wings as they leave.

Condor with full crop lands in tree east of our post at 1725. Swallows flock all around condor. Steve and I climbed steep hill, stopping several times to observe bird. Monty was at post watching through scope. Condor watched as Steve and I approached. At 1802 a red-tailed hawk swooped at the condor who hurriedly vacated perch and soared close over Monty, circling too low for him to get the whole bird in frame with his 500mm lens.

Harley Greiman and Carl Koford were stationed five miles from us on Tuesday but were unable to reach us by radio. At 1345 to 1400 hours, they saw three condors, two definite adults and one possible juvenile. We lost sight of condors at 1320 as they headed in general direction of their observation site.

Conclusion: This group now includes an immature. From the way it handles itself in air, it appears less adept than the others, perhaps fledged in late fall. We again observed possible pair bonding behavior of two apparent adult birds.

* * *

Wednesday, June 4-5. Escarpment w/Monty and Sanford Wilbur, U.S. Fish & Wildlife Service Biologist.

At 0930 we stopped before Base Camp and checked Escarpment, one condor roosting on rock ledge near our observation site on top. On to camp where we stored gear, then moved to top. At 1145 one adult over Gavilan Mt. 1152, a condor alighted in tree to the east, stayed until 1210, then soared over us and disappeared beyond a ridge to north. 1513, condor over West Roost rock. Although almost a mile away, we clearly saw it had a full crop. It circled and rose high to join another adult with a full crop. At 1608 a third condor with full crop circled over our position and the others landed on West Roost rock. Third condor soared to NE, then landed on a whitewashed rock on cliff face above Gavilan Canyon. Birds still roosting as we left.

Thursday

Condors active all day, flying, roosting in area. Sometimes three birds together, other times in pairs or soaring alone. No sign of dark-headed juvenile this trip. Sandy suggested it might have been older than we assumed and on its own rather than part of family group. Also, of three adults observed this trip, there was no definite pair. We saw interchange of partners on several occasions.

* * *

Saturday, June 21. Escarpment—alone.

Arrived at observation post at 1145 and checked all roosts. At 1215 I spotted one on Gavilan Canyon roost tree. Walked down to a meadow below and at 1445 two adults circled very low above observation post, then soared out and back to tree on high point at eastern end of Escarpment. Both landed on top branch and settled. A third condor flew in and circled tree. When this one tried to land with first two, they left. The new arrival pursued one, then was pursued. All three soared in circles and as they came overhead I could see all had full crops. As I walked back I stopped and glassed the Escarpment and Gavilan Mt. Three condors soaring over east ridge above Gavilan Canyon.

* * *

Tuesday, June 24-25. Escarpment w/Joseph Knowles, Jr.

We observed cycle tracks going from locked gate above Base Camp all the way to top. Packed Sham, my saddle horse, with equipment and overnight gear and moved on up to the observation site. Cycle tracks all the way. We unpacked cameras and scopes, then checked over edge for condors. Saw one across on Gavilan Canyon roost tree at 1052. We could see yellow-orange head in bright sun. Sky is clear, temperature 60°, light breeze. Bird left the tree and dropped out of sight into river drainage to the NW and did not reappear.

Cumulus clouds building to NE, fog boiling over mountains to west and a cold wind out of north. 1725, adult condor crosses escarpment to West Roost rock. As it circles low at base, another adult appeared almost immediately from around rock. Third condor is in front of Escarpment directly over observation post and moves to join them. Two landed on low outcrop and stood face-to-face, with a bobbing and weaving motion as they touched necks and heads. At times the birds displayed with wings outstretched to the first joint, primaries not extended, showing white underwing coverts. Display continued for seven minutes, then they sat quietly side by side. At 1747 they displayed again for three minutes. One flies off and other moves to a higher ledge. Wind is strong and second condor tries to land but cannot.

Wednesday

Strong wind has not abated, temperature is 37°. In place at our post by 0855, wind gusting up to 30 mph, air clear. We see snow-covered mountains, no condors.

45

One adult sighted on West Roost rock at 1354, another below. This bird disappears and reappears. Must be a ledge on far side of roost. Both adults grooming, running feathers through their beaks. 1412, both out of sight around West Roost.

At 1418, a condor to south. Appeared to lose its lift and was forced to flap heavily, wing beat of about one per second until it picked up an air current over Gavilan Canyon. We lost sight of it as it continued to lose altitude. Condor reappeared from north and circled over us, looking closely. We watched for ten minutes. This bird had a short new primary on each wing. It went out of sight, legs dangling, behind West Roost rock where others had gone.

* * *

Tuesday, July 22-23. Monolith Ridge and Escarpment w/Monty, Steve, Jerry.

Jerry and I checked Monolith Ridge area. No recent roosting or nesting sign. Monty and Steve had recorded a day of sightings from Escarpment post. Exerpts from Monty's notes:

"1030, adult condor from east. Circled and landed in snag. Red-tailed hawk harassing condor, probably caused it to abandon perch. White stripe visible on top portion of each wing, orange head. Landed on the high eastern rock, preened feathers, then with its back to sun, spread its wings. Noticed short new primaries on wings. 1130, still on roost and preening breast, wings and tail. Then at 1200, a second condor circled roosting bird and landed two feet from it. Began pecking and crowding it from roost, and followed it into air. Both flew out and back to rocks on a ridge farther east. I noticed condor on lower rock lay down, the first time I've seen this behavior.

"A pine tree due north of our post showed whitewash not present on past observation. Black beetle wing coverts in excrement on rocks below tree. Dick took sample to Museum of Natural History and the entomologist determined they were *Scarabicidae* family. Usually found in animal carcasses where they feed on hide, fur, feathers and dried tissue. They are beneficial scavengers and represent the last stages in the succession of organisms feeding on carcasses. No doubt ingested by condor while feeding."

Wednesday (Dick lost notebook)

Monty's notes continue:"1045, condor flew from east directly to same roost rock where we saw a bird land yesterday after being harassed by the red-tail. It has new short primaries. Dick has hiked out to check the area to the north and the roosting condor appears to have seen him, stretching its neck and watching him."

* * *

Tuesday, August 26-27. Escarpment—alone.

Checked Monolith Ridge area, no new sign. Looked at Escarpment from below . . . no sign of condors. At top by 1230, Gavilan Canyon trees clearly show new whitewash, no condors. Golden eagle at 1455. Saw bear cub tracks on way down.

Wednesday

No birds in sight. Note numbers of side-blotched lizards and Western fence swifts. They are completely unconcerned with the 1000 ft. drop at the edge, rush directly over rock, down the face and under overhangs. Violet-green swallows play in the breeze, making fast passes at speeds near 40 mph close to me. Seem to make a game of it. One or two sitting on a branch just back from the edge, fluffing feathers extensively and preening with their bills. The morning drags by with no sign of any large birds in air or on rocks.

I decided to check roost trees in Gavilan Canyon. Crawled through willow thicket, heavy brush . . . almost impassable. Took an hour to move ahead 700 ft. through dense dead scrub oak. Too dangerous to go any farther down alone . . . turned back. Will have to wait until others are along to try this.

* * *

Tuesday, October 21. Annual Condor Survey, Station: West Big Pine Mt. w/Monty. 45 posts in Southern and Central California reporting.

At lookout by 1007. Saw condor on tree in Big Pine Canyon, facing sun. Weather cool, medium wind but building. Official count started at 1200 hours. 1206, flock of 30 Clark's nutcrackers moved into the pines on the north slope of West Big Pine. 1640, two unidentified large, dark birds to the east, too far to identify.

47

1976

Friday, January 9-10. Escarpment w/Monty, Steve, Jan Hamber, Museum of Natural History, and Marty Hicks, USFS.

Jan and Steve to observation post, rest of us started to hike down to check Gavilan Canyon roost tree. Saw two condors on main rock below Escarpment post. We were more than a mile away but decided to go back. Condors gone by 1030 when we reached post. Soaring condors to south at 1045. 1047, Jan spotted condor below, flying with legs down. Then another with a yellow-orange head circled below. Both rose and flew east. Couldn't track them in light and shadow below horizon.

Three circling over North Peak, three and a half miles away. Out of sight at 1130. Now there are four high over the peak. Watched them until 1210.

At 1247, three condors in from the south, flying low and circling above us. One has dark head, spotted white underwings, white bar on wing tops. At least one adult has full crop. Total observation, uninterrupted flight, 55 minutes.

Saturday

No condors seen in morning. Decided to check Gavilan Canyon trees. 1230, walked down steeply descending pine ridge, following deer and bear tracks. Broke through dead brush until we could see snag tree ahead. Several lightning-struck trees have whitewash on limbs and the lowest of these is observable from our post on Escarpment. 150 ft. yellow pine, dead for at least 20-30 years and quite rotten at base. Found one body feather under it, 80 mm long. Tree above also had condor feathers below. No condors in air all day.

* * *

Wednesday, March 24. Escarpment w/Monty, Steve, Jan.

Moved rocks from road on way to Base Camp. Had to use sledge on some.

At 1400 we saw two condors on top of North Peak. Although more than four miles away we see them clearly. They sit, and walk back and forth. One drops off and down the face. We see several cavities in this formation.

We moved west on trail ¾ mi. from post. An adult condor from south. Looked us over, flew out over the valley . . . now in a straight line for North Peak. In view for five minutes, drops below skyline.

Earlier check of whitewashed cliff above Gavilan Canyon showed a dark shape we couldn't identify. Now at 1515, Jan saw a condor drop off top and fly to a perch just below. We can see whitewash shaded by brush in this dark hole. One or two birds somewhere on this cliff. Last check at 1630 . . . condor still in view on Gavilan Canyon cliff face.

Monty had been observing from western end of Escarpment. He saw a condor on a rock on Gavilan Mountain at 1308. This area not visible from our Escarpment post. Bird was a quarter mile from Monty's position and he noted it had a very red head. He whistled and bird left roost and circled over him. Condor had a full crop and third primary was missing from right wing. Second condor in sight but birds didn't appear to fly together.

Conclusion: Two condors sighted on North Peak and noted a number of potential nest or roost holes near top. Disappearance of condor into brush-shaded cleft or hole on Gavilan canyon cliff may be significant. Monty's observation of two condors unseen from our Escarpment post may indicate a second pair in area. We were seeing two on North Peak at same time he was watching two soaring birds.

* * *

Thursday, April 22-23. Escarpment w/Jan.

1614, single adult condor sighted on rock on face of Gavilan Canyon cliff. It sat there looking attentively in all directions, craning its neck this way and that . . . preened its ruff, twice opened its wings, sunning. Finally the bird left the perch, caught a lift of air, circled briefly then rose and headed over the valley.

Friday

Decided to check Gavilan Canyon area more closely. Hiked across one ridge, down a steep, deep draw, scrambled across a shale hillside, and over to a ridge where we could see the roost rocks on Gavilan

Canyon cliff. After studying the area with binoculars for two hours, we could see in the morning light a cavity that might be a nest hole. This is where we saw the condor roost during March observations. At 1123 a condor soared over from the south, crossed the canyon and rose high and circled twice before heading out of sight to the east. With bird gone and none on roost rocks, we hiked back to Escarpment. Condor at 1535 circled above us, then out over valley.

* * *

Tuesday, June 15-16. Escarpment w/Monty, Steve.

1010, condor roosting below at 5000 foot level. Monty looks over edge and says it has a bluish neck, white feet, black body, orange head. Bird is looking around, picking at feathers. It rubs its head across back with sort of a grand flopover turn. Sergeant's stripe shows clearly on wing. It goes under a ledge at 1100 and reappears with another adult. They circle for several minutes before returning under ledge. 1145, both fly up to the roost rock before moving to a double formation nearer our post. They seem to be watching us. We noted one has a red head with a large patch of dark feathers between the eyes and the other's head is lighter, orange, and has fewer feathers on face.

1145, red-headed bird leaves and the other sits for a while with the wind blowing its feathers. Then it chases a raven, using quick and aggressive maneuvers for a condor. At 1244 it circles down and goes back under the ledge. (This is where we observed a condor disappear on May 12, 1976.)

At 1433 an adult condor soars in from the southeast, circles above us at 300 feet and lands on the Twin Roost. Sits alone, looking around and preening. Seems the voyaging bird has returned. Now it chases away a raven, lands and then goes after a hawk. Condor from below joins it in air and now both are soaring at 1610 . . . truly magnificent! Coming together in air, we can see their white underwings clearly as they circle, legs down, bouncing in air as they obviously hit an air pocket. I'm watching upper bird, Monty the lower one through binoculars. Getting late, expect them to settle soon.

Now they are crisscrossing—BEAUTIFUL—spiralling above this canyon bottom, rising in an airlift here and there. Absolutely fabulous to see them soar. Beautiful birds moving so very slowly, majestically. It's amazing how long they can keep this up in such a tight deep canyon. Unlike the literature, their circles are tight. I'm following the red-headed bird, with a fifth left primary missing. Aha! it's chasing a

raven, now both are after it, right on it and the raven is ducking to get out of the way . . . fascinating to watch. Real vendetta against ravens, perhaps they are protecting a nesting area below.

Red head continues to circle as other goes beneath ledge at 1630. Now red head under ledge. Twenty-three minutes later both back on Twin Roost watching ravens. Red head goes below again, stays under ledge twenty-four minutes, back on rock at 1722. They move close, one aggressive and other moving away, they touch necks together, then sit quietly. 1800, cruising canyon bottom. Ravens are back . . . condors in hot pursuit. Now as red-headed bird flies to roost on tree above Gavilan Canyon, other disappears beneath the ledge at 1908.

Wednesday

Condor on Gavilan Canyon tree at 0840, assume it's been there all night. Bird is stretching and sunning wings. Dropped down from roost at 0910 and we lost sight of it. 1310, condor is suddenly on twin roost. It is the bird with lighter head . . . same one we saw disappear below last evening. 1329, it flexes its wings and drops below ledge again.

From the road we glassed face of the Escarpment six miles away and could faintly see a number of cavities in the area where birds have been disappearing.

* * *

Tuesday, July 13-14. Escarpment w/Monty, Jan.

Our first check of all roosts showed no condors. No activity until 1605 when we sighted a condor approaching from the northwest, moving fast. Appears to be an adult, red-orange head, but underwings are splotchy. Another condor rises and both now circle widely four miles out, then fly close to Escarpment and we see one of them has two loose primaries dangling. Suddenly comes a third condor from the south at 1613. This one has a black head. A juvenile! Now all three are ranging around the Escarpment and as they rise we observe how rapidly they flap their wings to keep airborne at over 7500 ft. By 1623 all are out of sight.

Wednesday

Monty stayed at Escarpment post while Jan and I hiked to Gavilan Canyon trees. Halfway down slope we see two adult condors on a dead sugar pine, one on a high branch, the other on branch below. We decided to continue slowly on down. Priscilla jumped a bear and went barking and crashing through the brush. Condors merely turned on perches to look. One bird has light orange head with almost no feathers on its face and the other shows heavy patch of feathers between eyes. They trade perches. We can see how their feet balance on the branches, not gripping. The top bird has a healthy appearance, black glossy feathers. It inflates its neck and cheeks. Lower bird seems thinner with duller feathers. I went a few hundred feet lower and took some photographs. Jan saw them crane their necks and look as I came back up, then they continued to preen and stretch their wings. Birds usually seen to leave this tree by 1000 so we wait. They fly off at 0953 and soon as they are out of sight we move down to base of the long dead snag. Found one secondary wing feather 44.5 cm long.

Monty had seen the birds on roost tree from the Escarpment post and was able to follow them once they flew. He watched them circle low over twin roost area several times before they moved out to the east. At 1845, we saw a pair of condors as they flapped and rose slowly from a valley near Monolith Ridge. We clearly saw birds had full crops.

Conclusion: Good possibility we saw five birds in two days. Pair seen on our way out did not seem to be the ones we saw this morning, might be the birds seen Tuesday. Roosting pair are the same ones seen June 15-16 showing interest in area under ledge below Escarpment. What was the juvenile seen yesterday? Where did it come from?

* * *

Saturday, July 24-25. Escarpment w/Jan.

Hiking out to Escarpment post we saw an adult condor showing a full crop heading toward Escarpment. When we reached the top at 1540 we found one bird moving restlessly on the West Roost rock. It settled down and stayed until 1808 when it moved to the edge to watch a bird we couldn't identify pass by. Now at 1819 a condor in sight for a moment against the sun and the bird we have been watching leaves the roost and soars out to where we lost sight of the bird coming in. Our bird glides out and back again and again, riding thermals . . . seems to be having the time of its life. It's hard to follow as it flies low against trees and rocks. It flips high into air . . . back and forth. Moving with apparent pleasure, legs down, almost rolling in air at times, soaring alone. Our arms are ready to drop, this is really concentrated observation, I don't dare look at the time. 1844, it is joined by another, they soar together, circling low, close together. 1848, red head lands on the Twin Roost rock and other on a snag just to east. Same pair we've been watching since June. Red head spreads wings . . . they're fantastic! Its head is turned back, wings curved, tips turned up, looks like the legendary Thunderbird. Settles for night . . . confirms our suspicions that something going on here. Will check again in August. At 1933, red head goes under ledge, in a minute the other condor is under ledge!

Sunday

At 0745 we see a condor on a tree on Gavilan Canyon slope. This is a Big Cone Spruce where we haven't seen condor use for a year. It is the red-headed condor with extensive feathering between its eyes. Jan dubs it "Groucho" because of its comic appearance. Groucho sat quietly until the sun hit its perch, then stretched its wings and sunned, moved to a top branch to better catch the morning sun. Can see he has food in crop. At 0948 bird moved from roost and at same time other condor appeared from ledge below us. They circled a while before landing on separate rocks. Lower one is Groucho. By 1034 both have landed somewhere on rock in front of Escarpment. 1044, birds suddenly back in air, circling, but we can't keep track. By 1111 a condor is seen on Twin Roost rock, other is out of sight. This is really an inaccessible area. We've been watching here for almost three years and there is no way to get down to check without breaking our necks. 1130, Groucho still on rock but leaves at 1135. Back on rock at 1147. We picked up the pack horse and headed down at 1202.

* * *

Monday, August 23 Escarpment w/Monty, Jan, Steve, et al.

Condor on Gavilan Canyon tree at 0910. Suddenly a condor appeared on Twin Roost at 0945. Bird on tree across canyon disappeared. New arrival sits quietly plucking at its feathers. Second condor lands at 1110 and they touch necks and bills while facing each other. Monty observes bluish color on their necks, while legs and feet appear white. Both show full crops. One is Groucho and Monty decides to call the other "Spot" because it has a circular bare spot in the scant feathering on its face. This is the pair we have been watching all spring. At times they pull down from their bodies and it floats away on the breeze. Monty counted 17 pieces of down in an hour.

At 1523 Groucho dropped down to ledge where we suspect there is a nest. Spot flew out of sight to the north at 1547. Groucho reappeared from under the ledge, soared high and was gone by 1601.

* * *

Tuesday, September 14-15. Escarpment w/Monty, Jan, John Borneman, DeLoy Esplin, USFS Biologist.

At 1400 an adult condor in sight below Escarpment. It circles the roosts, the possible nest site, then flaps and lands on the east twin rock briefly before dropping down under the ledge. Back out after three minutes and we can see it has a full crop as it circles 350 ft. above us. A second condor sweeps over ridge. This one shows an even larger crop. Its legs are lowered as it moves down and under ledge at 1430. We can see no change in size of its crop as it flies out from possible nest four minutes later and circles around the Escarpment, then spirals high to the south. At about 2000 ft. above us it sets its wings and glides down to twin rock at 1446.

Back under ledge and out again in six or seven minutes. Now the other has returned. These are the condors we've nicknamed Spot and Groucho. They soar together, ranging out and back over Escarpment area and we kept them in sight with scope and binoculars for 54 minutes. Then they land on trees above Gavilan Canyon and settle for the night.

Wednesday

Only one condor all day. In sight overhead at 1356, disappeared over North Peak in less than a minute. We arrived home late but pleased with trip observations. We're hopeful there may be a young bird in a nest. Agree to check from below.

* * *

Wednesday, October 13-14. Escarpment w/Monty, Jan.

Arrived at top after shoveling our way across a slide. At 1000 hours I stopped to check Escarpment, saw an adult condor sunning on one of the Big Cone Spruce adjacent to twin rock. Could see it only when it turned and showed white underwings, due to shadow behind and lack of a scope. Rushed to top by 1020. Condor still on tree. Monty was stationed on another peak and I called him on walkie-talkie, but he couldn't see the bird. I turned around and discovered it had flown.

We watched red-tailed hawks, golden eagles and a flock of thirty ravens high over Escarpment. No condors.

Thursday

Monty called in from his post to report a condor roosting on tree by Twin Roost. Same bird on same tree as yesterday, sitting with its ruff up around its neck. 1047, bird is airborne and suddenly there is a second condor, both are soaring high, then down below us. An immature golden eagle is seen . . . they're attacking! Their wingbeats and dips and turns in the air were as fast as those of the eagle as they chased it. Eagle reached out legs and talons and condor swerved to avoid them. Condors finally drove eagle out of area. One of the condors flew under an overhanging projection on the rock face and clung to the rock for a few moments. It was an unbelievable spot to try to land.

1059, both on Twin Roost, Spot and Groucho, sitting side by side. Now one leaves and we keep it in sight as it ranges to east until it is almost ten miles away. Other condor settles down on the rock as if to warm itself. Went under ledge at 1247 and stayed for almost two hours where we think there is a nest.

1600, one is back on the Twin Roost. 1645, another with a full crop circles over roosting condor and they both vanish under ledge. Out again at 1706, Spot and Groucho flying in close formation, soaring, dipping, circling apart, then meeting in air. Monty described it as an aerial ballet. Both overshot the roost tree, circled back and landed.

* * *

Saturday, October 23-24. w/Jan and Steve.

This special trip was planned to search out a better vantage to view the area where we have seen condors disappearing since May. We suspect there is an active nest somewhere on the Escarpment but don't wish to disturb the birds. Perhaps we can spy on them from below.

By 0845 gear is packed on my saddlehorse, Mocho. We take the trail to the west. At 1000 hours we can see the face of the Escarpment from the trail. Set up scope and sighted in on holes that show much whitewash around them. Too hazy to see clearly.

Long way off, about two miles, a bird is sunning. Possibly a young one—we are waiting for more light—are we seeing a young bird? Steve's turn at the scope, "It moved!" We look . . . it's a baby condor, not fully fledged! It moves about, flapping to hop up the rocks. Now it clumsily moves down into a low cavity and we lose it in shadow.

Twin rocks are to the left and we are looking directly at area below ledge where birds have been disappearing. Cliff almost vertical, nest appears halfway up. Impossible to check. Condor had been sunning with wings outstretched showing white underwings. Its head is light grey, downy. Body is black, only a 25-power eyepiece on scope, can't see much detail.

Steve and I hiked up a deep drainage from the trail to see if we could get closer. Looks like we could get to Big Cone roost trees but ledge with nest impossible to attain. Jan saw young one enter the lowest cavity. In about 15 minutes it came out as an adult condor suddenly came over a ridge from the north, dropped down, circled in front of young bird and then moved out of sight over a ridge to the north. Young condor watched, then back into shadows, hopping to keep its balance. Jan saw it attempt a short glide.

At 1625 it moves up to a second hole and is sitting on a white-washed promontory in front. It opens its wings. When they are stretched, the shortness of the primaries is obvious. Moves head around continuously, looking at everything. We can see faint band of lighter grey on top when it flexes wings. Young bird is agile but clumsy. Now boldly flaps to another rock several feet from holes, raising its wings and looking up into sky. No condors in sight. We left at 1700, reluctantly.

Sunday

Young condor on same ledge as last night. 1028, sky clear, no haze. Bird moves up to left of caves, stands tall and thin, gawky. An adult condor surprised us, moved in from south and landed with the baby who began flapping before we ever saw the adult coming in. We can't be sure if it's Spot, head looks quite light. Now the adult is feeding it ... like a tug of war ... still feeding six minutes later. Adult now moves about twelve feet away to edge of rock. Young one follows like a child testing its balance. Adult watches as the youngster moves around, then approaches. Feeds it again at 1330, baby flattened on ledge with wings pumping, adult bent over with head down. Now older bird is off, soaring close. Young one flapping, jumping up and down ... very precarious. Adult out of sight and young condor finally settles down. Calm and quiet now at 1345. Balances on edge and moves to lower ledge at 1415. Still roosting there when we leave at 1500 hours. Home by 2000 hours. Called Sandy Wilbur to report our find. Sorry Monty wasn't along!

* * *

Tuesday, November 2-6. To Sisquoc River w/Dennis Cogan to check old homesteads and Indian sites.

Left Cachuma Saddle at 1050 and reached Hell's Half Acre by lunchtime. Trip up easy and cool. Stratus clouds in light streaks, good breeze. Ate wild cherries growing along trail. Arrived at McKinley Spring at 1530. Sun already behind mountain and there's a chill in air. One hell of a pull after we left Hell's Half Acre. I rode a little. Both horses tired, had to rush them both the last two miles. Water here is great! Cold! Horses are under blankets, Polish sausage on the fire. Fall colors beginning, maple trees all around, water trough is full of leaves. All day we saw red-tailed hawks in pairs and ravens in bunches, trail showed old horse tracks and few fresh people tracks.

We're both tired. Only four hours of climbing, but steady. 1830. Sad, but it's time for bed. Temperature in 60s. Almost a full moon. Walked horses up to trailhead to feed, then back down for *monardella* tea. Quiet.

Wednesday

0630. Dennis saw a pygmy owl land in maple over water trough. It sat quiet as could be as we turned on flashlight, then flew. Reached Mission Pine Springs by 1030 after stopping to check Indian tool-making site. Camp is clean and neat. Tied horses to picket rope to feed on good meadow grass. 1125. I'm looking toward West Big Pine, can see it clearly. Condor in sight, very dim from here but definite. Walked to little canyon to north. Lots of water and deep little pools. Collected seeds of *Lilium pardalinum*. There are lots of giant mushrooms, some boletas.

Thursday

0710. Lots of *stipa* (bunch grass) along trail. Cooper Camp—found old whiskey bottle top, old granite ware. Walked up steep old trail, then slid down and had to walk way downstream to get back to where we had tied horses. Dennis still complaining about all we had eaten the night before. Trouble was an almost full moon. We ate too early, went to bed about 1830 and then horses wouldn't settle down. Mocho kept untying the knot with his teeth, wandering around. I had to get up each time. Both restless, not tired. Took them ten miles today. I went up to rocks and saw a condor over West Big Pine. We're very far away. Another roosting on a tree?

Friday

Watched sunrise from rocks. We'll check nearby areas today. Wild strawberry plants all over near springs. Woodrat has stored mush-rooms up in meadow. Stone pestle still in place by the cut trees, we hid it. This is a heavy acorn year, they're falling all over. Interesting day, exploring all around camp. Full moon tonight. Lots of deer tracks. Found a bear's bed in the little dry canyon just over the ridge, lots of bear scat. Horses were quiet last night. Didn't give them much to do today, hope they settle down. Nice fire, lantern lit. Good clear weather all day.

Oddly enough, the world appears void of people from Mission Pine Springs. We sat on the rocks in front of camp . . . can see San Marcos Pass. Streams of single lights. It is as though the entire population is a grand illusion. We can see the Topatopas and Santa Barbara Island—but no people. The solitude is absolute.

Saturday

Pack up and leave by 0815. Mountain quail calling all around. Hundreds of bandtails on way out. Picked a bunch of wild cherries at McKinley Springs to make jelly. Back at truck by 1345.

* * *

Thursday, November 18-19. Escarpment Nest Area w/Monty, Jan, Steve, Jim Hathaway, USFS.

Before we reached Base Camp we discovered a wheel problem on the USFS four-wheel drive vehicle. While we stopped for repairs, Jan and Monty glassed the Escarpment and at 0938 spotted the young condor on a rock. It is now apparent that the nest is visible from the road! Decided to split up; Monty to Escarpment observation post, Steve and Jim to west trail where we had been in October, Jan and I stayed at the road with the scope on nest area. 0951, the young condor jumped to a lower rock and then at 1001 it's flying! Bird flew about 700 ft. to the west, lit on promontory, then back to top of nest rock.

In the few weeks since we last saw it, the young one has learned to fly! It flies to Twin Roost rock. At 1017 it hops, flies straight out and down to nest. Thirty minutes later one of the adults, can't tell from this distance if it's Spot or Groucho, lands on Twin Roost and young bird flies up to it. While we moved the scope the adult left, joined second adult in air and both soared above the young condor on Twin Roost. By 1147 one is on a tree near West Roost rock and the other has landed on rock promontory just out from tree. 1200, both fly down to Twin Roost rock and youngster assumes a prone position as they circle close in front, but they move up and out to the east. I run down the road to see where they are going. One is over mountain to east, possibly foraging?

With three observation posts, two in radio contact, we are able to keep track of adults roosting and flying in the general area all day. From the road, we saw the adults suddenly land with the young one on top of nest rock at 1434. They seemed to just appear, but Monty had been watching them on West Roost rock and noted that they left at 1430 and made several passes over the young bird before landing. He saw the young condor being fed, then the parent nuzzled its wing. Young bird's head was down on rock and adult stepped on its head, then crowded it toward edge as if to say, "Get off and fly!" We watched them circle low over Monty on top of Escarpment for more than forty minutes after they left the young bird. They finally soared away to the northeast. Their youngster still sitting above the nest when we left.

Friday

Monty at observation post on road today, rest of party on top at Escarpment post. The young condor is sitting quietly on Twin Roost rock at 0735, its ruff is up, can see grey beak, fuzzy grey head. Wing feathers look shiny and new, wind is ruffling feathers. 1410, young bird hasn't moved except to change position and occasionally search the sky. No sign of Spot or Groucho yet. At 1520, young one flew down to nest rock. From 0735 to 1520, seven hours and forty-five minutes, we watched the young condor. Parents never showed up. Obviously doesn't need to be fed every day. Still roosting above nest as we pack up to leave.

A Forest Service patrolman, on way up road to replace destroyed NO MOTORIZED VEHICLES signs with metal ones, stopped to talk. He had chased fourteen bikers who had gotten beyond locked gate but couldn't cite them because wooden signs were down. Bikers have carefully constructed path around gate and we saw tracks of at least three two-wheel vehicles going all the way to top. Patrolman pointed out where Forest Service had put out a lightning-strike fire in a yucca. They actually put a crew on south slope near the nest site by helicopter in late October. This is an outrageous violation of the Critical Habitat!

* * *

Thursday, December 9-10. Escarpment w/Monty, Jan.

Checked nest site from road but no sign of young condor. Noted no action on gate construction, cycles still using by-pass. This was reported in November! Unloaded our gear at Base Camp. New cycle tracks on trail to top. Stopped to check south face of Escarpment and at 0927 observe an adult showing a full crop and the young bird. They are on a whitewashed rock just below the top. Young one nuzzles the adult bird's crop and beak. Adult responds by forcing the immature's head down on the rock, then takes off into the strong cold wind spilling over from the north. Moments later the immature bird soared out and down toward the nest. Amazing flying capability in this heavy wind!

1123, adult condor in sight. Young bird joins it in air. They are circling above nest canyon . . . looks like a flying lesson. Adult flies to east and the youngster lands on one of the twin rocks. We watched sky to north and when we looked back were surprised to see Spot and Groucho with the young bird on Twin Roost at 1325. Monty saw them land. Adults entwined necks together, then one opened its wings fully and strutted back and forth in courtship behavior. A time or two it curved its wings forward around the other, engulfing it . . . almost like an embrace. We notice the jowls on the older birds as they turn away. Young bird appears thin-headed.

1405, young bird has been facing adults, now it puts its head down almost between its legs. Wind ruffles its feathers. Now it reaches out and pushes against an adult's crop, but the parent responds by pecking its head. At 1443 both of the adults have flown, leaving immature on twin rock. By 1520 young bird gone, probably down to nest.

Friday

Monty to lookout. We walked down to check possible condor

61

bathing pools. Passed a waterfall, running strong and fringed with ice. Mushrooms on trees and ground, lots of fresh grass. Ladybugs. Trees and brush quite heavy. Saw no open pools suitable for condors.

John Borneman came up to Escarpment where Monty was observing. At 0955 they saw the immature condor fly from the nest site up to a rock below the Twin Roost. After a while it lay down on the rock. Monty says, "Like a chicken." The bird flew at 1025 and was met in the air by one of the adults and both went out of sight. Back at 1110 circling and gaining altitude. Young bird moving well in a thermal.

Now soaring alone at 1126, it's very adept at flying. As it circles, the white underwings show some dark feathers. Lands on a high rock, possibly where we first saw it yesterday morning. An adult, looks like Groucho, lands with him. Both have their ruffs up. Through the 80-power Questar, the tip of the adult's beak appears quite white. Leaves roost, flying low and out of sight to the east.

At 1300 an adult condor, harassed by an immature golden eagle, heads towards roost and lands with the young condor. Now the eagle struck at the immature bird and the adult jumped up to meet the eagle's rush as it dove at the youngster from behind. Condor almost fell, but managed to get airborne with the eagle right behind, still chasing. Condor flew back to the rock, seems to feel safer there. Harassment continued for another five minutes before the eagle finally left the area.

Young bird sitting erect with wings drooping. Adult bird showed extensive red on head and neck after the excitement. Though hard to see from his position, Monty decided it was Spot, and could see the orange showing on breast, indicating this bird had food in its crop. The youngster extended wings toward the sun, then stood with one wing spread.

Both birds in air at 1412, circling on thermal, young one flapping unsurely, following adult. Then it soared alone, circling, occasionally flapping wings. Awe-inspiring to see this new young condor testing its wings.

1977

Thursday, January 20. Check Escarpment area w/Jan.

0940. Light rain, temperature 49°F. Heavy clouds building overhead. Looks doubtful that birds will be in air today. We walked up the fuelbreak. Sighted red-tailed hawks, white-throated swifts. No condors seen all day.

EDITOR'S NOTE

This is the last entry in Dick Smith's condor journal. On February 2, 1977 he died of a sudden heart attack. In the early evening he staked Sham and Mocho below their corral to graze the fresh new grass coming up after the rains. He probably ran back up the steep hill as he always did. He seemed to rush through life. Back of his home a lightbulb glowed under a plastic cover, providing warmth to set the fiberglass repair he had just made on a friend's saddletree. It dimly lit what was meant to be a patio, now cluttered with tools, sawhorses, saddle stands and half-finished rawhide braiding projects. He lay just beyond the light, stopped in mid-stride.

The condor watch goes on. The Museum of Natural History and the Forest Service cooperate to continue the study he initiated. The information he gathered will be part of the museum archives and with the new observations will add to a better understanding of the magnificently ugly birds he cared for. They symbolize the persistence of life. A man is only noticed in passing by these great Ice Age survivors. They may circle above and peer at him curiously before moving on. One man doesn't matter, but his caring must go on.

In May 1977 an immature condor was seen roosting with one of the parent birds not far from the nest site. Then in August, yet another recently hatched condor ventured from the same nest cave and teetered about on the precarious ledge and was fed by Spot and Groucho. By October it was already flying short distances.

Young condors have been reported from this remote area since 1972, a year before Dick and Jerry Berry came upon the black-headed juvenile on Monolith Ridge as they searched for Indian cave paintings. This 1977 youngster, already flying so early, is all the more remarkable because it is the offspring of a vigorous pair of condors that seem to nest yearly. Read again the field notes from April 1, 1975. We can only speculate whether Dick was describing the same birds Jan and Monty eventually nick-named Spot and Groucho. A dying species! In the late 1960s a pair of condors nested in the Hi Mountain area of San Luis Obispo County and successfully hatched young for four consecutive years, rearing them to the flying stage. No way has been devised to follow the progress of the young ones once they are on their own. No official program exists to locate and study nesting condors on a continuing and scientific basis. Statistics and demographics are compiled from random sightings and projections of the relatively few valid studies made since the 1930s. How can decisions be made when so little is known! "Experts" speak of a senescent species, of waning reproductive vigor, as they plan "last ditch" programs of intervention to save the condors.

Meanwhile, a pair of condors soars over a wild remote land. They follow nature's pattern as new condors are hatched, cared for, and taught to fly. Do the flocks that forage the ranges of modern cattle ranches where herd animals are scientifically bred and fed reproduce! No one really knows, but many are beginning to question as Dick did, whether this vaccinated, supplementally fed and hormone injected food supply disrupts delicate mechanisms of the condor's breeding cycle. Each new discovery and added bit of information and observation raises new and perplexing questions.

What we already know of the California condor makes a fascinating history. Unanswered questions remain a challenge for future members of the condor watch.

—OLIVE KINGSTON SMITH

Groucho and Spot on Roost Tree.

Stretching wings in the sun.

Condor country—the San Rafaels.

Whistling wings.

Vigilant.

Perched on a Big-cone Spruce.

Part II

CALIFORNIA CONDOR
Its History, Mythology and Reality

BIRD AND SYMBOL

At eight o'clock on a summer morning, an enormous dark bird spreads his wings, flaps with powerful, deliberate strokes and rises from a nesting ledge on the face of a waterfall cliff. He soars on the lifting air currents to a mile above Southern California's citrus groves and oil fields. In widening circles, he passes high over sprawling subdivisions and missile installations, remote cattle ranches and busy freeways. He is *Gymnogyps californianus,* the largest North American bird that flies. His body is as heavy as that of a year old child, and the span of each great wing would reach higher than the shoulder of a tall man.

He has been soaring for almost half an hour, but his wings have not moved since he left his perch. He circles once more to get his bearings as his mate, circling below, rises to join him.

She is indistinguishable from the male for she is nearly as large, her plumage and markings almost identical. Their bare heads and necks are a red-orange color, their eyes are also red, brilliant. The powerful beaks are the color of dark horn. A ruff of spiky black feathers circles the base of their necks and can be raised for warmth or to make their appearance more formidable. A band of white feathers crosses the back of each wing below the shoulder and larger triangular-shaped patches of white mark the undersides of the wings, stretching from close to the body and tapering to the wrist joints. Their greyish legs and feet fold back close under their tails in a V as they soar.

Flying several hundred feet apart the birds now line out to the north, away from civilization toward the foothills along the San Joaquin and Salinas Valleys. Near Paso Robles, Shandon, or inland toward Bakersfield, or farther north to Porterville and Visalia—forty, perhaps fifty airline miles away—they will find food.

They start back home in midafternoon. They have fed on the carcass of a large Hereford calf already partly consumed by golden eagles and other scavengers on a remote grazing range. Their crops are full and distended. The covering red skin bulges in the breast feathers below their ruffs.

Near San Luis Obispo they encounter dark thunderclouds reaching high into the sky. They veer east to catch the rising currents of sea breeze deflected upward by the coastal mountains, and circling even higher, they fly on above the storm.

Just east of Santa Maria they descend toward the Sierra Madre Ridge, a flyway their kind has known since their ancestors soared above the receding ice sheets. This ridge runs generally from northwest to southeast, ideally situated to deflect the cool ocean air and the hot thermals rising from the arid brush-filled canyons of the interior.

A cowboy astride his horse high on Miranda Pine Mountain looks skyward as the birds come hurtling out of the blue distance like two jet planes. They dip low, peer at him curiously, turning their heads as they pass above. Their giant wings whistle with a rushing sound as they level out and speed along the ridge. It is like the sound of a wind through pine trees.

Farther along, a man exploring a deserted forest road, grabs his gun and opens his car door. He has never seen a bird so large. Unaware that it is illegal to shoot at any vulture-like bird, he raises the rifle. Before he can take aim, they have gone by, cruising over the crest and out of sight.

It is late afternoon when they reach the ledge on the waterfall cliff where their nestling waits. The chick is four months old. The first black feathers have appeared in the grey down that covers his body. Helpless and awkward, he leaves the nest only to waddle about on the precarious ledge and watch the sky for the familiar shapes to appear.

The pair alight and greet him, nuzzling and nibbling him gently, putting off for the moment his feeding. The small wings flap as he begs with soft hisses and grunts. The female lowers her head and stretches her neck toward the young bird. The male then leaves the nest cave and moves to a rock perch near the top of the cliff. The food in his crop will feed the chick the following morning.

The excited chick thrusts his head into the mother's open beak and begins to feed. Again and again their heads join in the feeding until he has had his fill and is quiet. Then the female leaves and flies to the pool above the waterfall. Her mate joins her.

Together they cross the sand and wade into the water to drink. They take quick nibbles at the clear stream and raise their heads after each sip to swallow as chickens do. They bathe, sloshing the leading edges of their wings and dipping their necks to let water stream over their backs. Once or twice they nibble at each other with apparent affection, then they shake the drops from their feathers. A large rock to the west of the waterfall glows in the last rays of the sun and they hop onto it and spread their wings wide—so wide the spread seems unbelievably enormous, eight, nine, almost ten feet—they extend themselves and relax in the fading warmth. At dark they drop through the air to roost.

These are California condors, living in this quiet moment as condors have lived since Stone-age man came to inhabit what is now the southern part of the United States.

The history of the condor is linked with the history of man in western North America. Condor bones are found in ancient caves and burials. Living condors were sacred to prehistoric man, and in remote caves and on sheltered rock walls his painted image flies through the centuries in evidence of forgotten ritual. God-symbol, bird of life and death, he soars from timeless legend to today's reality. His fascinating history holds a message for modern man ... and a powerful implication for the future.

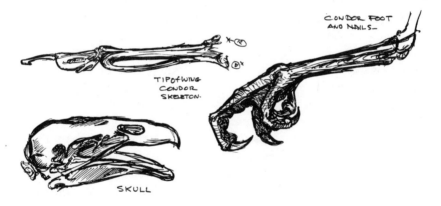

CONDOR FOOT AND NAILS

TIP of WING CONDOR SKELETON.

SKULL

IN THE BEGINNING

Condors have been flying as long as man has lived on earth. Origins of the bird are frozen in the strands of geologic time. Fossil records 60 million years old found in Wyoming indicate there was, even then, a specialized winged vertebrate whose purpose was to transform carrion to living material. Though that ancient bird is extinct, its descendants came winging on to fill that vital role.

Earliest man shared his kill with a giant-winged vulture scientists call *Teratornis incredibilis. Teratornis* was related to modern condors. He had a wingspread of approximately 17 feet and was probably the largest bird ever to fly. Great dark birds cast a shadow of fear and awe wherever primitive man struggled to survive. *Teratornis* and the Pleistocene condor, *Gymnogyps amplus*, may well have inspired supernatural images, the terrible and unbelievable aspects of power from above that haunt the collective memory of mankind.

These relatives and ancestors of modern condors shared the earth with saber-toothed cats, dire wolves and the huge short-faced bears. They and lesser predators, prehistoric man among them, stalked and fed on mastodon and woolly mammoth, camels and tiny antelope, great herbivores, small mammals—and each other.

From tar pits, cave deposits and archeological excavations we can trace the whistling wings of modern condor and his ancestors.

Imagine the area now covered by the sprawling city of Los Angeles and its environs. See a land rumbling with earthquake, exuding liquid petroleum, stifling gases, and boiling hot springs. A sunburned plain that stretches from mountain range to foggy coast is bathed with a reddish haze as the afternoon sun moves across the sky. It is already late in the day and a band of naked hunters, their rude spears held ready, watch slow swirls of dust rise where a herd of primitive antelope graze uneasily.

Unseen by the hunters, a saber-toothed cat stalks in the shadows of a nearby ridge, intent upon easier prey. A cow camel nudges her new-born calf and it lurches to its feet and stands on wobbly legs.

High overhead, obscured in the dust and haze that lifts with the rising thermals, an enormous dark bird circles. With watchful telescopic eye the condor has caught the double game of life and death unfolding below. His circle narrows . . . he waits.

The stalking cat strikes. A sudden flurry, a startled shriek . . . and the calf is pulled to the ground. The camel dashes onto the plain calling the alarm and the herd of tiny pronghorns scatter as she whirls and rushes back. Confused, the men draw back and watch as the saber-tooth feeds. Soon his hunger is satisfied and he leaves.

Cautiously now, the Stone-age hunters emerge from their hiding places glancing sideways to be sure the great predator is gone, and advance upon the carcass. Shadows suddenly block the sun and the sky is filled with huge dark birds circling down. It is the black shroud of nature's death watch.

In awe and anger, the hunters hesitate as the birds descend on the mangled carcass. But the men's hunger is strong and they rush forward to claim a share. The birds reluctantly retreat and stand silently beyond the reach of the spears and watch. The condors' turn will come. They wait.

In fitful sleep, the hunters may then dream of saber-toothed cat and giant vultures, creatures that animate the darkness and linger to haunt their waking thoughts. In time they will become man's legends, symbols of awesome powers of life and death. And man will speak to them in ritual and sacrifice as he attempts to placate and direct his universe. Condor bones have been found ritually interred with early human remains.

For 50,000 years on the North American continent the condor ruled the skies and gripped the minds of men.

Now man has become a lordly creature. He no longer goes naked or wraps himself in skins. He dresses in fashion and his countenance is sharp and sure. His weapons boom like thunder and animals live on or die at his whim. Great mechanical birds now dominate the heavens and man levels the mountains and diverts the life-giving rivers with technology.

And the condor still lives on. In small scraps of yet untouched land, he follows the ancient ways ... and waits.

RITUAL AND MYTH
The Condor Dance

"We have killed the bird chief. Now we are going to take him home. Our chief will announce a fiesta to honor this bird chief."
—Gifford, Central Miwok Ceremonies

The *Molokbe* (condor impersonator) is ready to perform the *moloku* (Condor Dance). He enters the chief's hut where the singer or drummer helps him pull on a feathered condor skin. He pushes his legs through holes in the stretched skin where the bird's legs had been and he laces the skin up the front of his body. The great wings are tied to his arms and his head protrudes through the neck opening. The tail feathers drag on the ground.

The dancer's face is painted with a broad band of red, circling forehead and chin. His hair is bound with a net and a very long flicker feather headband crosses his brow, projecting far out to the sides. Two small feather ornaments *(sonolu)* rise on an angle, one at each side of his head. A feather ornament *(makki)* is jabbed into his hair and points forward from the crown of his head.

As the three performers march from the chief's hut, the singer begins the song of the dance. Singer and drummer enter the ceremonial hut while the dancer waits outside until the music begins. Then he enters and moves counterclockwise around the interior, peering from side to side, his wings hanging down. He pretends not to see the chief and the elders as he circles the hut. When he reaches the drum for the second time, he stops and stands motionless. The song also stops.

In a moment the singer resumes his song, accompanied by the drum. The *molokbe* dances slowly, his body moving up and down as he flexes his knees, circling the hut counterclockwise. He turns in various directions and raises his wings, imitating flight.

Every few moments he makes a hissing noise, imitating the sound of the condor. He glances from side to side as he bends far forward and then stands erect.

He circles the house four times, stopping at the drum each time. Outside, the people wait. Low moaning and wailing rise from the

76

women. The atmosphere is charged with mounting tension.

As the dance continues, the dancer seats himself upon the drum after each circuit of the hut and carefully arranges the condor's tail behind him so not to crush it. He raises the wings but does not spread them wide.

After a few moments the dancer rises and walks around the hut again, this time without music. He stops in front of the drum and dances back and forth as singer and drummer resume the chant. He raises his wings together, then alternately, as he bows and rises.

The *molokbe* prepares to leave the ceremonial hut and dances counterclockwise toward the outer world where members of the tribe are waiting. Midway, he stops and the drummer exclaims as before while the dancer kneels and faces the sacred fire, beating the ground with his wings.

The drummer pounds hard as the dancer slowly rises. This performance is repeated near the door and he dances to the fire for the last time. Now, as he moves backward, each wing is alternately raised and lowered. The drummer shouts "Heh! Heh! Heh!"

This is from a description of an actual ceremony performed by the Central Miwok Indians of California. It characterizes the condor-impersonating dances of many tribes in the once-wide range of the condor. Some tribes perform similar ceremonies even today.

It is evident the California condor was an important part of Mourning ceremonies. Often the bird was sacrificed during the ritual and his spirit set free to travel to the upper world.

Tribes who had access to a condor nest usually cared for a young condor for several months prior to the ceremony which occurred in the summer or early fall. Throughout most of California, these captive birds were considered to be the property of the chief, although it was the custom for the person who had actually found the young condor to receive payment from the chief.

The nestling was taken in April or May and was thus five or six months old at the time of sacrifice. The young condor was fattened and made much of by its captors, indulged as a sacrificial victim-to-be and as a representative of the supernatural being.

After the ritual killing, the bird's skin was carefully removed. Sometimes it was stuffed with straw. Other tribes preserved the skin as a garment to be used in the dance and they buried the body inside the sacred enclosure with various seeds sprinkled upon it. Usually, only the feathers were saved. They were carefully plucked, made into capes, skirts, and headbands, and used to decorate the tops of sacred poles used in rituals honoring the sun and the dead.

Some, among them the Central Miwok Indians, hunted the condor for sacrifice, and usually the bird was killed by one of the chief's hunters. The bird was immediately skinned and its body burned. The men danced around it as it burned, scattering *tuyu* seed upon the fire and singing to the dead bird chief. Then the condor skin was stretched on sticks and carried back to the village where deer marrow was rubbed into it to make it soft. The chief arranged for the ceremony to be held which would ensure his people's well-being. If this was not performed, the Indians believed the chief or the hunter, or their families, would be stricken with disease.

Perhaps the earliest account of the California Indian's association with the condor as a religious symbol is found in the diary of the Franciscan father, Juan Crespí, who traveled with the Spanish explorer, Portolá, and an overland party moving northward from San Diego in 1769.

When the Spaniards made camp on the evening of October 8, they were near an Indian village on the banks of a small river approximately a hundred miles south of what is now San Francisco. Fr. Crespí wrote: "We saw in this place a bird which the heathen had killed and stuffed with straw: to some of our party it looked like a royal eagle. It was measured from tip to tip of the wings and found to measure eleven spans. For this reason the soldiers called the stream Rio del Pájaro . . ." The river bears the name Pájaro to this day.

The bird seen by the Portolá expedition may have been a sacrificed young condor, although they did not report witnessing a ceremony involving the bird. The village had been burned and was deserted when the party reached it. Later observers recorded these rites in detail as occurring in such widely separated localities as the Sacramento Valley and San Juan Capistrano Mission.

An indispensable part of these ceremonies was a skirt or a cape made from the feathers of the California condor. Feathers were also made into headbands. Many tribes destroyed ritual garments by burning or interment upon the death of the dancer or shaman who owned them, and today few examples of these costumes remain. Cave deposits and other ancient relics indicate that even condor feathers were sometimes spliced together for greater length. Perhaps

78

ceremonies seen by early Spaniards were derived from rituals of prehistoric man. The two-foot long condor feathers fastened together may have indicated a tradition and mythology of the giant *Teratornis incredibilis,* passed down for centuries.

Father Geronimo Boscana, a Franciscan priest at Mission San Juan Capistrano, recorded the sacred condor ceremony of the Acagchemem Indians, who lived near the mission in the early 1800s. They are known today as the Luiseño-Juaneño.

The most celebrated of all their annual feasts they called the *Panes,* bird feast. They held particular adoration for a bird resembling the common buzzard or vulture, but of larger dimensions. The day selected for the feast was made known to the public on the evening previous to its celebration, and preparations were made immediately for the erection of their *Vanquech* (temple, or sacred enclosure). On the opening of the festival, they carried the *Panes* in solemn procession and placed it upon the altar erected for that purpose. Then, immediately, all the young, married and unmarried females, commenced running to and fro, with great rapidity; some in one direction and some in another, more like distracted than rational beings; continuing thus racing, as it were, whilst the elder class of both sexes remained silent spectators to the scene. The *Puplem,* (shamans and those with supernatural power), painted as heretofore described, looked like so many devils, in the meantime dancing around their adored *Panes.*

These ceremonies being concluded, they seized the bird and carried him in procession to the principal *Vanquech,* all the assembly uniting in the grand display—the *Puplem* preceding the same, dancing and singing. Arriving there, they killed the bird without losing a particle of its blood. The skin was removed entire, as a relic, or for the purpose of making their festival garment, *paelt* (skirt). The carcass they interred within the temple in a hole previously prepared, around which all the old women stood, weeping and moaning most bitterly and throwing upon it various kinds of seeds and particles of food, exclaiming at the same time, "Why did you run away? Would you not have been better with us? You would have made pinole as we do, and if you had not run away, you would have not become a *Panes.*" Other expressions equal in simplicity were made use of and, as the ceremony was concluding, dancing commenced again and continued for three days and nights, accompanied with all the brutalities to which they are subject.

The Indians state that said *Panes* was once a female who ran off and retired to the mountains, when accidentally meeting with CHINIGCHINICH (Great Spirit) he changed her into a bird. The belief is that notwithstanding they sacrificed it every year, she became again animated and returned to her home among the mountains. But the ridiculous fable does not end here; for they believed, as often as the bird was killed, it became multiplied; because every year all the Capitanes (Chiefs) celebrated the same feast of *Panes*, and were firm in the opinion that the birds sacrificed were but one and the same female. They had no evidence, however, of where she lived, or where she originated, and neither were the names of her parents known. The commemoration of the festival was in compliance with commands given by *Chinigchinich*.

California Indian religion was difficult for the European to comprehend. What the Spanish and later Anglo settlers dismissed as rituals of heathen people in reality expressed a system of belief that encompassed all of the Indians' natural surroundings. All living creatures, as well as rocks and mountains, trees and plants—everything perceived—was related to human survival. Each was a source of power to be used for the common good, power that could be acquired with ritual and ceremony. Stars and planets in their travels through the sky influenced the daily life of the Indian and he could communicate with them through visions and magical acts.

As a supernatural being in the religions of many California Indian groups, the condor was represented as possessing various powers in different roles. To the Chumash of the southern California coast he was *Holhol*, one of the Sky People, clothed in feathers and carrying two beautifully wrought sticks which he struck together first before and then behind his legs in order to travel great distances quickly. His magical clothing and sticks contained power that enabled the user to locate missing persons and to find lost objects. Neighboring tribes knew him under other names in similar roles.

Some believed it was the condor who held the Upper World aloft on his wings and caused solar and lunar eclipses, not the eagle as many tribes commonly believed.

To other groups, the condor was a human who had been transformed as in the "Panes" described by Fr. Boscana. For the Eastern Pomo of the northern California coast, he was *Sul*, formerly a great dancer. Knowing that upon his death he would become a bird, *Sul* instructed his people and gave permission to be hunted and killed. His feathers were to be used when the *sul ke* (Condor Dance) was performed.

The Tlingit people of the northern Pacific coast said the condor made the thunder with the flapping of his great wings, and lightning flashed from his red eyes.

In remote and almost inaccessible places, far from now-forgotten Indian villages, painted condors and painted figures of men adorned with condor feathers endure in ancient ritual images.

Most if not all Indian pictographs in Southern California seem to have been sacred. A cave high in the arid wilderness of the San Rafael Mountains appears to have been the scene of important religious rites. Within the darkness of the sandstone cave, strange figures and symbols are painted with red, black, and white pigments on the smoke-blackened rock. A hole has been painstakingly drilled into the cave wall and extends four or five inches through the rock to the outside. As the sun rises over Hurricane Deck on December 21, the day of the Winter Solstice, the first rays are blocked by an outcropping fifty feet to the east of the cave. When the sun beams across the crest of this formation, a shaft of light enters the cave through the small man-made opening. It strikes the floor of the cave below a rare realistic painting of a condor. In a ceremony to arrest the shortening days of winter, a sacred sunstick, adorned with condor feathers, may have been erected in the earth where the sun's rays first struck the cave floor.

The head of the condor is painted with the red iron oxide prized by the Indians. Wings, feet, tail and body are of natural white calcium. The bird itself is soaring up out of the mouth of the cave, drawn on the living rock of the upper lip of the entrance. The condor is about to take flight into the high clear air of the backcountry. He is symbolic of the ascending hopes of men, and is rendered in colors that have lasted until today.

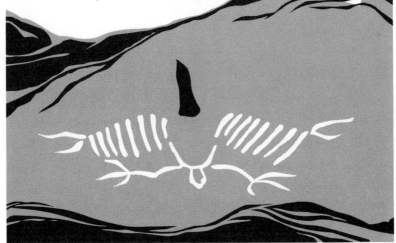

10'

CONDOR   ADULT

CONDOR   JUVENILE

GOLDEN EAGLE   ADULT

GOLDEN EAGLE   IMMATURE

TURKEY VULTURE   ADULT

FACT AND FICTION

Something akin to superstitious fear crept into the minds of many early white settlers when they saw the California condor. Large birds, dark birds, dark feathers were traditionally associated with witchcraft, evil and things supernatural.

Whatever the specific reason, many Western pioneers regarded condors as dangerous, ill-omened, carriers of disease, or just generally harmful. Many early settlers were convinced that condors attacked living cattle and sheep, carried off calves and lambs, even infants and small children. Actual cases of eagles attacking children and domesticated animals were readily attributed to condors. Reports of South American condors attacking live sheep and calves—which has happened—were intermingled. As a consequence, the big dark bird that flew in the sky of the West was often thought bad.

There is, of course, no basis in fact for the belief that California condors attack or carry off live animals or humans. The condor's feet resemble those of a turkey and have nails rather than talons. They are not adapted for gripping and rending. The condor uses his beak to grip and tear his food.

Condors can perform prodigies of strength by using bills and feet. One early account states, "Four condors dragged off for 200 yards the body of a young grizzly weighing upwards of 100 pounds." But another account claiming that a condor flew off with a hindquarter of venison is false. There are no substantiated accounts of condors flying off with anything.

A popular bit of condor lore is that miners in the West and in Mexico used condor quills as containers for gold dust. The light durable quills could each hold as much as ten cubic centimeters of fine dust, worth roughly $105 at 1855 prices. They had a diameter of nearly one-half inch. Each quill was fitted with a wooden stopper and had an attached thong so it could be worn around the neck. A man with a necklace of three or four quills could be carrying a modest fortune. And where else could you find a container so durable, waterproof, and handy in frontier times?

Stories of the condor's misbehavior were widespread. From the human's point of view they were often true. Andrew Jackson Grayson, living in 1847 in the mountains of Marin County near what is now called Mount Tamalpais, told of a typical hunting experience. He had shot a fat buck, dragged the carcass under some bushes and scanned the sky to be sure no condors or buzzards were near, then went home to fetch a horse to pack out the meat. When he returned an hour later he found a dozen condors devouring his buck and another dozen or so circling above.

No doubt Grayson and others in similar circumstances opened fire on the birds. A man who hunted to feed himself and his family felt no compunction about destroying any animal that threatened his livelihood.

To the pioneers, the condor was thus sometimes a nuisance, sometimes costly, and in yarns told around campfires he was made to appear a terrible menace.

It was often thought that condors carried disease. This belief doubtless arose from the bird's association with carrion, but there is no evidence that condors carry diseases harmful to humans or domesticated animals. Nevertheless, many of the big birds were killed for this reason.

Condors will overeat to the extent that they have difficulty becoming airborne. A full bird may need as much as 30 or 40 feet of runway and sometimes a favoring slope to get off the ground. Spanish ranchers were able to capture the birds by placing carcasses of sheep or cattle inside pens or small corrals. A hungry condor could alight, but gorged, he could not readily take off again. Vaqueros, as well as later cowboys, often lassoed them for sport out on the open range when they came upon birds logy after feeding.

This writer observed a grown condor barely able to take off after feeding on the carcass of a horse. Like an overloaded plane, he was able to fly only to the top of a fifteen-foot pine stump a few yards away. He perched there for more than an hour while being photographed from the base of the stump. It is evident that condors could easily have been captured or killed by men or animals at such vulnerable moments.

Condors have been tamed and there are many recorded accounts of them as pets. Harley Wells, who lived in the upper Sisquoc River area in Southern California in the early 1900s, had a pet condor who followed him around at the end of a string. The Wells children played with the ungainly captive much as they played with other pets.

Perhaps the best known pet condor was W.L. Finley's young bird,

84

General. It was taken from a nest in Southern California more than half a century ago, reared in Oregon, and finally made its home in a New York zoo where it lived to a ripe old age. Finley could play with General and the bird would respond with affectionate nuzzling and gentle nibbles. One of their favorite games was tug-o'-war with a piece of rope. Finley likened General to a loyal dog or horse. Many other condor owners have testified to the same gentle qualities in their pet birds.

Between 1901 and 1903, the National Zoological Park in Washington, D.C. received three live condors from California. In May, 1924, Joseph Dixon of the Museum of Vertebrate Zoology at Berkeley, visited the park. He wrote: "The Condors constituted to me the chief attraction in the park. Three fine adult examples there live in a spacious 'flying' enclosure. Although now twenty-one and twenty-three years old, these Condors appear to be in the prime of life ... There is no strife; all three birds live together in real harmony." He further reported on the breeding and nesting behavior of the condors: "Ned Hollister, Superintendent of the Park, has furnished me with the following data. The captive Condors bred for the first time when they were twelve years old. The birds have 'nested' three times ... In each case, the single egg was laid upon the bare wooden floor of a large shelter or roost which was placed well above the ground. In every instance the egg proved to be infertile." The birds lived until just before World War II.

The gigantic size of the condor was a typical tall tale of the West. In a time and place that tended to exaggeration, the condor was not overlooked. Fourteen feet was the usual measurement given as wingspread. James Clyman, well-known frontiersman, twice recorded birds of this size, and Clyman was a fairly reliable observer in most respects. The *Daily Alta California,* San Francisco's leading newspaper in the 1850s, reported a condor of fourteen-foot wingspread that not only impressed the editors but allegedly flew off carrying a nine-pound rabbit. South American condors in this same period were commonly being reported with wingspreads of fifteen feet. Authorities now believe all these reports exaggerated, at least they have never been authenticated. Perhaps there *were* gigantic birds hidden in the fastnesses of the Andes and Coast Range in those days, or perhaps the enthusiasm of men got the better of their judgment.

Could there have been larger condors a hundred years ago? Conceivably. Given a larger sampling of any species, you are apt to find more oversize members. Therefore in early days, when the birds were more abundant, there may have been bigger specimens than today. Even now adult wingspread may vary as much as 12 to 15 inches. However, no birds reliably measured at any time have had a span as large as 14 feet. Most adult condors are in the 9 to 10½ foot range.

The greatest wingspread recorded in any substantiated account is reported from Santa Barbara County in 1908. The bird was taken on Loma Pelona Potrero by Arthur Wilcox, a member of the Cooper Ornithological Club, the oldest and most distinguished group of scientific bird enthusiasts in the western United States. Wilcox's bird measured 11 feet 4 inches from wingtip to wingtip and weighed 26 pounds.

Is, then, the California condor the largest bird that flies? So far as wingspread and body weight are concerned, he is and he isn't. A large wild turkey may weigh more. Some authorities claim that the Andean condor has a wider wingspread. Others claim that the wandering albatross "with a wingspread in excess of eleven feet" has the widest span. It is safe to say that the California condor may exceed 11 feet in wingspread, and that when combined wingspread and body weight are considered he may very well be the largest bird that flies, certainly the largest on the North American Continent.

It is also true that condors are long-lived birds. The greatest recorded age was forty-five years for a captive bird in the National Zoo. Since we lack knowledge concerning the life span of free-living condors, we can only speculate, but some authorities feel the birds may live as long as seventy-five years.

Inoffensive to mankind, this remarkable bird has suffered greatly from man's ignorance, superstition and intolerance. Even the knowledge we now have concerning the California condor has been gained at great cost to his numbers. Man has been, and continues to be, the deciding factor in the survival of this ancient species.

RECORDS OF OBSERVATION

Recorded history of the California condor begins in the chronicles of the first white explorers in the New World.

Cabrillo, Drake, and other Europeans undoubtedly saw condors in California in the 1500s but no records of observations have survived, until 1602.

Three tiny sailing ships are making their way north along the central California coast. They are dwarfed by towering cliffs and jagged mountains as they feel their way slowly into new water and a new land. On the deck of the *Santo Tomas* stands a Carmelite friar, Antonio de la Ascensión, chronicler and spiritual advisor of the Sebastian Vizcaíno Expedition which had been ordered by the Viceroy of New Spain to explore the coast of the Californias.

Father Ascensión recorded at great length the animal life seen by the party as they explored the region around the Puerto de Monterrey. His diary states:

"There are some other birds of the shape of turkeys, the largest I saw on this voyage. From the point of one wing to that of the other it was found to measure seventeen spans."

He was a keen observer and his measurement of seventeen spans, 11 feet 4 inches, may well be the actual measurement of a condor which he was able to examine closely. He had noted that there was the carcass of a dead whale on the beach and that bears came at night to feed upon it. Perhaps condors also fed upon this great source of food. When feeding in large groups, condors often seem fairly oblivious to man's approach. His measurement, considered by some to be exaggerated, though more reasonable than the fourteen foot wingspread so often claimed by later American pioneers, exactly matches Arthur Wilcox's specimen from Santa Barbara in 1908.

And so the myth of a great bird was given substance. Here in California, "an island at the right hand of the Indies," as many people then believed, the impossible was probably true. According to legend, California was a golden place where the only metal was gold and the only inhabitants women, ruled over by a queen named Califerne, who tamed wild beasts in golden harnesses. Therefore why not a giant griffin, a mythical beast with the wings and head of a bird, as had been hinted at by the earliest explorers in the New World.

Father Ascensión's account became part of a famous book, *Monarchia Indiana,* a monumental history compiled by the Franciscan scholar Torquemada, and published in Seville in 1615. Thus the existence of the fabulous great bird "of the Indies" became known to Europe.

A hundred and sixty years pass. The condor soars the skies undisturbed. He serves as object of reverence and sacrifice in Indian ceremony and his plumage is used in the ritual garment and sacred decoration. This undoubtedly serves as some check on his numbers, but there are so many of him that the loss is insignificant. Given all the ages of time, the Indians probably would not have exterminated the condor any more than they would have exterminated the carrier pigeon or snowy egret, or the vast herds of buffalo. A hundred and sixty years pass and no white man sees the great bird until 1769 when Pedro Fages, second in command of the Portolá expedition, records the Indian's use of the condor. Fages saw live birds as well as the stuffed one he described on the banks of the Pajaro River near the present site of Watsonville. He says the Indians domesticated "eaglets" in their villages but did not eat them, and gives the wingspread of the adult bird as "fifteen spans." A span was reckoned at eight inches and Fages' figure, about ten feet, is evidently accurate. Fray Juan Crespí, missionary, and Miguel Constanso, engineer, as well as Fages, all recorded information about the various sightings of the condor as the Portolá expedition made its way overland in its attempt to rediscover Monterey Bay.

From now on sightings become frequent. In 1792, Archibald Menzies, English botanist and collector, sails into Monterey Bay with the Vancouver expedition. He collects a specimen (dead) of the condor which is to become the official scientific type for the species and may still be seen in the reference collection at the British Museum.

During this period while the Spanish and then the English explorers were making their way up the Pacific coast in increasing numbers, ships flying the flag of Russia made their way down the coast from Alaska. Too little is known of their scientific observations and attempts to establish colonies on this continent, but in 1968, the director of the Oregon Historical Society visited a number of Russian museums. In Leningrad's Museum of Curiosity, he saw on exhibit an Indian cape made of condor feathers as well as one of eagle feathers. Perhaps in time, records of the Russians' early condor observations and contact with the Indians from whom these ritual garments were obtained, will be available to add to our knowledge of the California condor.

Enter the Americans. Patrick Gass, an Army sergeant with the Lewis and Clark expedition, was the first American to publish an account of the expedition. Gass' Journal appeared in 1807 and said:

"Wednesday 20th (November, 1805, mouth of Columbia River). They (Captain Clark and party) killed a remarkably large buzzard, of a species different from any I had seen. It was 9 feet across the wings, and 3 feet 10 inches from bill to tail.

"Sunday 16th (March, 1806, winter quarters about 30 miles from the mouth of the Columbia River). Yesterday while I was absent, getting our meat home, one of the hunters killed two vultures, the largest fowls I have ever seen. I never saw such as these except on the Columbia River and the sea coast."

When it was published in 1814, Lewis and Clark's account fully augmented Gass' brief description of the condor. Lewis and Clark encountered the condor as far east as the Wind River country of Oregon. They believed it to be the largest bird in North America and saw so many as they proceeded west they called it "the beautiful buzzard of the Columbia." They weighed one at 25 pounds. Lewis' accurate description of a living bird, accompanying a remarkably precise drawing of the head, was the first detailed record ever made of a live California condor.

Condors continued to abound and were frequently sighted in the Columbia River region in the 1820s and 30s, especially in the late summer and fall when they fed upon dead salmon near falls and along the river bank. They were seen four hundred miles inland, in present Idaho.

In 1827 the Scottish botanist David Douglas killed two specimen condors near the present site of the city of Portland, Oregon, and sent their skins to England. Douglas, who did not live to return to England himself, was regrettably less than scientific when he included in his otherwise accurate account, "Observations on the Vultur Californianus of Shaw," a bit of romanticized misinformation provided by a Canadian voyageur: "They build their nests in the thickest part of the forest, invariably choosing the most secret and impenetrable situations and build on the pine tree a nest of dead sticks and grass; have only two young at a time; egg very large (fully larger than a goose-egg), nearly a perfect circle and of a uniform jet black." Unfortunately this misinformation continued to be reprinted and used by other writers for many years, long after the nest and egg of the condor had been finally found and described by reliable observers.

In the early 1840s, John C. Frémont observed condors during his explorations of the far west. E.L. Kern, artist and ornithologist with several of Frémont's expeditions, collected the first adult condor to reach an American museum. Specimens taken by earlier collectors had been sent to museums in Europe, although the partial skin of a bird with juvenal plumage which was taken in the Columbia River region by John Kirk Townsend is still preserved in Washington, D.C.

Frontiersman Clyman, mentioned earlier, recorded in his diary: "Napper Creek, California, August 16, 1845. We had rare sport shooting deer, Bringing in the skins in the Evening, the most of the meat being left on the ground for the wolves and vultures and of the latter the country seems to be remarkably well stocked. Beside the raven and Turkey Buzzard of the states you see here the royal vulture in greate abundance ... "

Early observers continued to describe condors in superlatives: "the most majestic bird in flight ... ", "The magnate of the air ... ", "magnificent ... incredible ... ", and they shot them in ever increasing numbers.

John James Audubon had a special ambition to travel west and see the California condor. He was never able to do so and his well known color plate of the bird was drawn from sketches furnished by ornithologists who had seen live condors, though it is possible he may have had specimens to work from. His autobiographical notes indicate that in spring 1835 he completed thirty-three drawings while in London and he writes of his gratitude to the Council of the Zoological Society of London for providing him with American species from their collection, even allowing him to take them to his house. Among these American species were the condors collected by Douglas, so it is possible that Audubon was able to use these to complete his famous drawings.

Audubon's second son, John Woodhouse Audubon, was able to travel to California. He tramped many weary miles in hopes of not only seeing a live condor, but of observing the nest and downy young of the "California vulture." The nature and location of condor nests remained one of the mysteries of the naturalist world.

John W. Audubon did achieve his goal of seeing the great bird of the West and even believed he had observed a nest. He made sketches to accompany his observations, and he followed his studies with a devotion comparable to his father's as this passage from his Western Journal shows:

"April 9th (1850) This morning we crossed the river (Tuolomne) and after a trot of about five miles, came to the canyon. I made my way to the lower end called Indian Bluff and my sketch was finished by probably five o'clock, but having no watch I cannot tell. Here I saw the nests of the California Vulture, but on the opposite side of the river, now an impassable current."

However the nests in question were not condor nests, as subsequent entries in Audubon's journal make clear. Condors do not nest in trees in the manner Audubon describes, and he observed no birds or eggs to prove these nests exceptions to the rule.

By the late 1800s, sightings such as the Canadian ornithologist, John Fannin's two condors in British Columbia, and that of Herbert Brown who reported a condor killed near Pierce's Ferry, Arizona, were considered rarities.

One of the most gripping early observations of a collector's concern, and his utter disregard for the safety of the bird, is this account that appeared in 1906:

"Then it was evident we could not scare (the mother condor) from her den. But we had to have a picture of this baby bird, the nestling of the largest bird that flies, and one that is so rare in the ornithological world. Crawling over closer where I could look through the crevice in the rock, I got down within three feet of the mother as she sat covering her chick."

The collector could see white on the big bird's shoulder, in fact he was close enough to touch her. The blood-red eyes watching him must have been a little disconcerting as he gathered up the courage to reach in to get the chick. At this point the bird drew back as if to strike and the man quickly flipped the chick toward him with a small stick he had in his hand. Once the chick was captured he looked back and "the mother sat in sullen and accusing silence."

The man and his companion quickly set up the camera and tripod in the, by then, pelting rain and took pictures of the chick in a spot protected by a bit of overhanging rock. After each two or three time exposures, one of the men would pick up the chick to warm it. Finally they realized the chick was becoming dangerously chilled so they returned it to the nest. To their chagrin, the mother condor ignored the overhandled chick which had now grown too weak to even squirm ... "I knew the chick would die if it were not accepted ..." Again the intruders warmed the nestling and at last ... "she suddenly recognized her nestling, putting her bill down, drew him gently near, tucking him carefully under her breast. We slid back out of sight, and began the steep descent."

"In the condor home far back in the mountains, I saw the display of a deeper love and affection than I have ever seen in my life," one of them wrote.

It seems clear that until the First World War, the condor was considered a rare and remarkable sight, worth mentioning in detail. One should remember that these were the great days of "nature loving" when America discovered its outdoor heritage of wildlife and wilderness, days of Muir, Seton, Theodore Roosevelt, and also a time when almost every boy dreamed of growing up to be a hunter or trapper. To shoot birds and animals and rob nests and dens was a "normal" experience, and often had as great an element of curiosity in it as vandalism. Museums and zoos were establishing collections, taking many specimens. It was an age of natural discovery as well as of exploitation.

The best close description of a live wild condor is perhaps that of W.L. Finley who, in the decade before 1914, observed a pair of adult condors from a distance of a few feet:

"Their bills were of dark horn color and the red skin of the head extended down covering the bill about half way. The feet were of similar color, but on each knee was a patch of red. There was a brighter patch of red on the breast of the birds, which could occasionally be seen when they were preening and when they spread their breast feathers. Both had light-colored wing-bars and the primaries were well worn. The skin on the throat hung loose and the lower mandible fitted in close under the upper, giving the bird a peculiar expression. The chin was orange and below this on the neck was a strip of greenish-yellow merging into brighter orange on the sides and back of the neck. The top and front of the head were bright red, but between the eyes was a small patch of black feathers, and these extended down in front of the eye till they faded in the orange red of the neck. The pupil of the eye was black, but the iris was deep red and conspicuous. The top of the head was wrinkled as if with age. The ruff, or long shiny black feathers about the neck, was often ruffled up, giving the birds a savage appearance. Behind the ruff in the back the feathers were edged with dark brown."

The adult birds repeatedly came within six feet of Finley with seeming absence of fear, after he had established the familiarity of his presence close to their nest and fledgling.

Finley, an ornithologist of wide interest in many species of birds, studied the condor's home life at close range over a period of several months and concluded: "I never saw a greater show of affection in any bird than the two condors seemed to have for each other and for their young. The longer we studied and the more we watched this family, the stronger our own attachment became for the birds."

The First World War, the rise of industrialism and affluence, urbanization and the automobile, coupled with the near disappearance of condors, served to turn men's minds away from the bird which seemed to be associated with another era. The condor's historical connection with man seems broken at this point. Records of observations dwindle to nearly nothing in the 20s.

Then in the early 1930s attention was once again drawn to the bird. The interest was particularly keen in Santa Barbara County as reports of condors in flight and feeding on carcasses began to appear in print.

A blind was dug within camera range of the carcass of a dead horse placed in a known flyway to attract the birds. Many excellent photographs made at this time are among the best record we have of the species. These pictures taken by Kathleen Dougan Hoover and Ernest I. Dyer are represented in a number of private and library collections.

Dyer, an amateur photographer and a member of the Cooper Ornithological Society, made careful observations of the birds at their feeding and nesting sites and contributed significantly to modern information about the bird and its dwindling numbers. A similar contribution was made by J.R. Pemberton who set up a blind in the Cuyama Valley and made the first extensive color motion pictures of the condor.

Another observation, some years later and from a new vantage point—an airplane—bears repeating: "On October 15, 1940 at 1:30 p.m., the writer caught sight of two very large soaring birds while piloting a two-place Cessna airplane above Liebre Gulch, about 8 miles southeast of Sandberg, Los Angeles County, and 26 miles southeast of Mt. Pinos. A lookout for Condors had been kept during regular weekly trips over this region since the preceding November, during which time many Turkey Vultures and a few Golden Eagles had been seen, but no birds as large as those now sighted. They were soaring at an altitude about 500 feet higher than the plane, the latter registering 5500 feet above sea level.

"A few seconds after altering course and climbing to approach the birds directly, I was able to identify them unmistakably as California Condors . . . As the plane overtook the Condors from their left, they behaved like other large birds of prey. They sailed to the right in a tight circle on motionless wings so that I was obliged to bank steeply to avoid running past them . . . "

The pilot, Lowell Sumner, of the National Park Service, stated that the birds became agitated when approached closely. They flapped their wings laboriously, made tight turns and when having success-fully out-maneuvered the plane, resumed their leisurely flight.

The first thorough and authentic study of the condor was made by Carl Koford of the Museum of Vertebrate Zoology of the University of California over a period of years in the late 1930s and mid-40s. The results of Koford's work were published by the National Audubon Society in 1953 and are a cornerstone in knowledge of the condor. C.S. Robinson, Assistant Supervisor of Los Padres National Forest, also collected valuable data derived from first-hand observations during the 30s and 40s; and the extensive field studies by the McMillan brothers, Ian and Eben, over the past two generations constitute probably the longest continuous observations of the bird.

In 1965, the National Audubon Society, and the National Geographic Society, with assistance from the Museum of Vertebrate Zoology of the University of California, published *The Current Status and Welfare of the California Condor* by Alden Miller and the McMillans. This comprehensive study further updated the knowledge of the birds, as well as giving an indication of the population at that time.

Today many agencies, both state and federal, together with national conservation groups, have initiated programs of study and education. Their combined efforts have resulted in more complete documentation of sightings, conservation programs, and protection of the birds and their habitats.

The enthusiasm of dedicated "Bird Watchers" can sometimes have its humorous side, for "Birders" often go to what other people see as ludicrous extremes in order to see a particular bird—especially one so rare as a condor. For example, when condors were reported on a ranch near Santa Barbara some years ago, a convoy of open cars was quickly formed. They arrived at the ranch in Santa Ynez Valley in short order and, tense with expectancy, the group proceeded in a column almost bumper to bumper through the pasture where the condors were supposed to be. No condors! Tension mounted. Binoculars raised. Suddenly a bird flew over. The first car stopped abruptly. Sixteen cars piled up, as the cars bumped, back in sequence to the last one, drivers and passengers intent upon the sight of the incredible bird. Luckily no one was hurt but most likely anyone in the expedition that day would have shed blood gladly for sight of that condor.

THE DEATH ROAD

After 1850 and settlement of the West, decline of the condor was rapid. Here is a typical example:

Alonzo Winship, later a pony express rider on the plains, surprised a condor asleep on the ground at the foot of a cliff near his Sierra cabin in 1854. "Surprised that the bird had not been awakened by his footsteps," reads the newspaper account, "Winship hesitated a moment, then decided to attempt to kill the bird. Having nothing but his shovel he threw it with all his force, striking the condor and breaking its wing."

Condors virtually disappeared from the Columbia River region by 1860. Men shot them. Few sightings were made in Oregon after that period. The "beautiful buzzard of the Columbia," as Lewis and Clark called him, was a thing of the past in the American Northwest. Virgin forests, grizzly bear and buffalo, all were disappearing as the white man spread across the land.

Early settlers were busy wresting a living in this new country. They did not bother to think much about the condor; they ignored or killed him.

Indians and Mexicans learned to join in the slaughter. "Every Indian and Mexican gold miner [in Lower California]," states a record from the 1880s, "is provided with from one to six of the primary quills of this species for carrying gold dust, the open end being corked with a plug of soft wood and the primitive purse hung from the neck by a buckskin string. All the dead birds I saw in Lower California had been killed for their quills alone." Condors then ranged for 200 miles below the border, their central habitats being the high peaks and rugged canyons of the Sierra San Pedro Mártir. Their primary quills which had been worth a dollar apiece in Alta California gold rush days were now worth nearly as much in Baja California. Condors died to serve the gold rush. Man was and remained the chief offender.

"I saw a condor perched in a dead tree not far from camp. I went for my gun . . ." reads account after account. It is a wonder any birds survived at all.

California passed a law in the 1880s prohibiting the killing of condors, but it received little publicity and next to no enforcement. And it did not apply to "scientific collecting," an apt and available title for any and all depredations.

96

In 1899, Lt. F. Ruiz, a surveyor, and his assistant were running a line up San Roque Canyon, not far behind the Santa Barbara Mission compound. They saw a condor on a cliff face 150 feet above them. Ruiz and his companion thought the bird might have a nest, so they made their way up the rock, peeked into a crevice and saw the bird crouched beside an egg on the floor of the hollow. "The bird remained in this position until I had thrown several rocks at it," Ruiz stated, then he and his friend retrieved the egg and started down the canyon. The mother bird, meanwhile, had flown from the nest and was joined by her mate, and the two birds followed above the men with the egg for a considerable distance.

Unnerving as this may have been for Ruiz and his companion, they did not put the egg back. Oologists (egg collectors) were willing to pay well for a condor egg for their collections. H.R. Taylor proclaimed in an 1895 issue of *Nidiologist* that he stood ready and eager to pay $250 apiece for up to three eggs of the California condor. Probably the highest price ever paid for an egg was $300 received by Kelly Truesdale in the early 1900s.

Condors continued to diminish. At best they are not prolific. They do not mate until they are at least five or six years old, perhaps as old as twelve or fourteen. They usually do not lay their single egg every year, but perhaps only on alternate years, or at even longer intervals. The young do not leave the nest until they are nearly a year old. Add persecution by man to the natural hazards that can interfere with successful mating, nesting, and rearing of young, and it is not hard to understand why the condor decreased so rapidly from the large numbers seen in the upper Salinas, Santa Ynez, Los Alamos, and San Joaquin Valleys of California within the memory of living man. "I've seen the Los Alamos Valley black with condors," says Guadalupe Mendoza, former vaquero on the Sisquoc Ranch. There was a time when ranch hands throughout Southern California could make similar statements.

Lack of food was not a major factor in the bird's decline. The condor had thrived before the arrival of vast herds of cattle and sheep, and had survived periods of drought when deer and elk, even squirrels and rabbits, may have died off drastically. He remained in balance with nature and was not dependent, for example, on the tons of meat left to rot on California ranges during Spanish rancho times when cattle were killed for their hides alone. This was a bonus, not the natural, hard-sought food the condor had been accustomed to for thousands of years. There probably has always been an adequate supply of food for condors. The problem for the birds today is an ever shrinking foraging range as urbanization spreads over Southern California, with once wild areas now being used for mass recreation.

The question arises as to whether the mass poisoning of ground squirrels and other wild animals in the late 1800s and early 1900s might have had an adverse effect on the condor population. The evidence is uncertain. Condors, like other vulturine birds, appear remarkably impervious to poisons that have spelled death to many other animals. Their systems are naturally resistant to toxic effects.

One apparently authentic instance of poisoning, however, was related by a Fresno County sheepherder in January of 1890. Manuel Cadoza brought two large condors into the town of Huron after he found them dead near the poisoned carcasses of a pair of sheep baited for coyotes. A number of condors had come down to feed on the sheep the day before, and on the following morning he found the two dead birds nearby.

Several unexplained condor deaths in the 1950s and 1960s were investigated by the McMillan brothers. All occurred in areas in Kern County where rodent and predator control programs were under way, and while these deaths were never officially verified as being poison caused, the Miller-McMillan report states that evidence points to poison as a contributing factor.

An ailing condor was discovered near Los Alamos, Santa Barbara County, in 1966 not far from the carcass of a calf poison-baited for coyotes. Unable to fly, it was taken to the Los Angeles Zoo where it was force fed and treated with antibiotics. The bird recovered and was successfully released a week or so later.

Evidently twentieth century man's introduction of chemical poisons, herbicides and pesticides into the environment is a factor that must be considered in the continuing decline of the condor population. Concentrations of toxic chemical compounds such as DDT, DDE, and other organochlorines have been found in dead condors recently. Analysis of the feather composition of a captive bird in the Los Angeles Zoo has shown an increase in nine years of 1,000% in the amount of mercury, 40% of lead, and 60% of zinc. Comparison of recent eggshell fragments with those collected before 1950 has shown structural differences and considerably thinning. Chemical compounds may be to blame. Contamination of food supply may be upsetting the delicate hormone balance necessary for the birds to breed. Research is continuing in an effort to determine whether man's pollution of the environment is proving too much for even the condor's strong constitution.

Nevertheless, the central cause for the condor's decline by the turn of the century was man's greed and shortsightedness rather than his use of poison.

"I was out on a hunting trip after deer, with a party of three Santa Monica boys and a rancher who was to guide us . . . I noticed an adult vulture (condor) perched about 25 feet below us . . . We watched her for a few minutes, then tried to scare her by shouting at her, but she would not take wing. We then threw stones at her but they all fell short, striking the cliff below her perch. At last the rancher proposed I should shoot at the cliff near her but I declined, saying that he had better do so, as his rifle was smaller than mine. I cautioned him to be careful not to hit her . . . He raised his rifle and fired and I was surprised to see her go tumbling down the cliff . . ."

At this point the hunter decided the condor's skin might be of some value so he made his way down the cliff face until he found the wounded bird ". . . full of fight with one wing crippled. After a hard tussle with her, I succeeded in killing her by driving the heavy blade of my knife into her brain . . ."

By 1910 experts had given up the species as lost. Only the remaining impenetrable and remote areas of the Coast Range protected the condor from immediate extinction.

Sweating up densely overgrown canyons, up nearly impassable dry waterfalls, across precarious ledges by hand and by rope, the thirsty, exhausted humans recorded the terrible, wonderful remoteness of these last hiding places. The condor had literally retreated to the heart of the wilderness. Here where remain the last vestiges of the flora of the Pleistocene era—spruce, cedar and horsetail fern—here, where there are still the silences and solitude of the earth before man, the bird too remained—for the moment.

Condors and red men had gotten along very well. Condors and white men did not. There is something unreasonable about a condor. The bird has to be comprehended, rather than analyzed. The majesty of the primitive ages is in him, as he comes winging out of the Ice Age, the majesties of the silences that were before man, and perhaps will be after him. One visualizes, too, the dignity of the slow procession of the eons of time. Since the rocks were laid down and the seas receded, and man first appeared on earth, this bird has been flying. His history may be irrevocably intermingled with that of man. The condor of mid-twentieth century that flew out from his last retreats soared over a changed and changing land.

Bulldozers had been invented. Four-wheel-drive vehicles had been perfected. Low-gear-ratio motorized vehicles designed for trail and cross-country travel were on the drawing boards. Helicopters and planes were flying. The end of World War II released these devices—and man's energy and attention and money—toward "developing" and "exploiting" what remained of our wild lands. Progress was still defined by many, even by government agencies, in terms of new roads and more gashed hillsides. Every untouched spot appeared a challenge.

Motorized vehicles came snorting up toward the last wild places, shattering the stillness. For the first time it became possible to take a machine almost anywhere, even to level the mountains if man willed. There was also an increasing feeling of "what of it?" if wilderness and condor died. "These lands belong to the people." Man's will must be served. If the Pleistocene Age was obsolete, so maybe was the condor. But at the same time there was an ever-increasing feeling among many people that something had to be done to save both condor and wilderness, that they both belonged to the people—the people for all time to come—people who ought to have a chance to know wilderness and condor as they are now and always have been.

Topatopa in the San Diego Zoo.

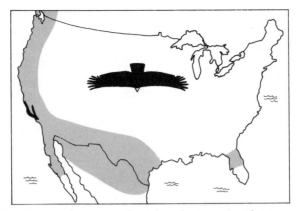

How the condor's range has shrunk since the Pleistocene.

THE CONDOR TODAY

Condor. The word is Spanish from the Peruvian *cuntur,* the native name for the bird. Perhaps it was brought to California like the pepper tree and walnut by seafarers. There was frequent and intelligent contact between California and Peru in early days. Certainly California Spanish people had local names for the bird. To the vaqueros around old Fort Tejon eighty years ago he was "wietro." Mexicans in California or Mexico were apt to call him a "queleli," while natives of Lower California referred to him as "buitre." To Californians of English-speaking background he was usually called "the California vulture" or "big buzzard," or "royal vulture." The term condor was little used even in scientific articles until the later 1800s, and the American Ornithologists Union did not use the term until 1931. The Indians of the southern San Joaquin Valley called him a "wee-itch." Most likely the name condor was gradually imposed through scientific, magazine, and newspaper usage.

No matter what he is popularly called, the California condor is a separate species officially known as *Gymnogyps californianus,* literally "the bald vulture of California."

He is reliably reported as larger than the South American condor as he weighs more. Both species have about the same wingspread. Both are members of the almost unbelievably durable and long-lived family of vultures that has come down through the centuries changing more slowly than most other living things. The condors flying today over Southern California's missile launching pads are but little different from the birds that circled over mammoth and mastodon, saber-toothed tiger, and Stone-age man.

Condors range from the edge of the Los Angeles metropolitan area northward along the Coast Range and the western foothills of the Sierra Nevada. Once they ranged from Canada to Mexico and across the southern portion of the United States. Now the northern limit of their range is roughly a line drawn across California between Fresno, San Jose and the Pacific Ocean. They are no longer seen east of the Sierras. Reports of condor sightings in the Sierra San Pedro Mártir area of Baja California in recent years remain unconfirmed.

They roost regularly not far from Visalia and are seen in the rangelands of Kern and Tulare Counties. These and the Sespe Creek-Piru Creek areas of Ventura and Los Angeles Counties, and the San Rafael Wilderness of Santa Barbara County are the main habitat areas today.

The birds often range as far as fifty airline miles to forage. They may not travel daily because sometimes they do not feed intensively for as long as a week after a heavy feeding. But when they do travel far afield they use the ancient flyways up along the Sierran foothills where they catch the up-drafts of the prevailing westerly winds and of the warm rising valley air, or along the Coast Range through Santa Barbara and San Luis Obispo Counties where the sea breeze is likewise thrust up by the land to create powerful thermal uplifts.

To sense the close passage of a traveling condor is an experience out of this world. You are riding up a trail at sunset, twenty miles from the nearest human settlement and you see racing toward you out of the sun's disc a great dark spot growing larger and larger with incredible speed. You realize it is a big dark bird. Suddenly he looms above you, peering down with age-old rather remote gaze. His eyes seem to have seen so much more than mere men that he appears only mildly interested. To feel the presence of that vast composure and to hear the rush and whistle of his feathers through the air, and to see him gone to his home in the darkening east, having passed within a rope's cast of you, is something to be forever remembered.

Despite their seeming composure, condors are insatiably curious. They like to investigate. You may see one soaring high above you. All at once he's larger and lower—just above your head, without seeming to have done anything at all to come down so quickly. This curiosity has often proved disastrous to the birds, because the temptation to shoot at anything that moves or flies is still overpowering in some people with guns. Nevertheless condors may still be seen in flocks of fairly large numbers. The record-high sighting was 43 in one flock on the Tejon Ranch in the mountains south of Bakersfield in 1947. A flock of 18 condors observed on the Tejon Ranch in 1972 constitutes the largest sighting in recent years.

A condor flies like most birds by action of air moving across its wings and causing an upward force or lift. But the outstanding characteristic of the condor is its ability to soar. This soaring is remarkable. Condors have been observed to soar for nearly an hour without flapping their wings. In soaring the wings are extended fully at right angles to the body except at the very tips where they curve slightly forward. The large primary feathers or "balancers" at the tips of the wings are separated by pronounced air spaces or slots, one slot being nearly a third of the wing in length. These wing slots are thought to be safety devices. As a wing increases its angle relative to a horizontal plane, lift and drag are increased. Beyond a certain angle, the air stream will break away from the wing's upper surface, in the effect called "burbling," and thus lifting power is lost and the wing is said to stall. The slots affect air flow in such a way that the wing will continue to have lifting power beyond the normal stalling angle. Thus a condor can soar without moving its wings.

In descending, a slot in the leading edge of the condor's wings, similar to that on an aircraft's wings, helps slow the descent while offering enough sustained lift to prevent a stall.

Ratio of the span of the condor's wing to its width is approximately 6 to 1. The narrower wing of the wandering albatross, for example, achieves more lift, yet the broader-winged condor's amazing primary

103

feathers just described compensate for the less efficient lifting power of the broad wing itself by controlling air flow in such a way that air does not slide out from under the wing at the tip causing loss of lifting power.

Aeronautical engineers have studied the condor's flight dynamics, and have found that the bird flies according to certain soaring principles. It is the habit of the condor to fly in circles, for example, when not traveling to a destination, and these circles have been timed to average 15 seconds. Condors often circle as many as 15 times in succession while gaining altitude, usually changing the direction of the circles before completing the entire number. Their large tails are used especially for steering and braking when coming in for a landing.

The condor usually flaps only in taking off, landing (as brake), in air where there is no updraft, or when fleeing or pursuing. He has been observed making headway into strong winds, has been clocked at 55 miles per hour in straight gliding flight, and has been seen to climb higher than 15,000 feet to fly above storms. One observer claims a speed of more than 100 miles per hour during a flight of 50 miles. Three thousand feet above ground is their normal altitude from which to begin long glides. When actively searching for food condors usually fly about 500 feet above ground.

Included in the official report on condors in the 1930s was the following observation by C.S. Robinson, Assistant Supervisor of the then Santa Barbara National Forest:

"An interesting experience in August 1937 gave an idea of the rate of speed while flying. Driving along the Cuyama road (State Route 166) a condor was noticed flying parallel to the road at about 2,000 feet elevation. Luckily the road was straight east for about six miles, and so we paced each other nicely at 45 miles per hour for nearly four miles before a turn in the road changed my direction. The condor gradually forged ahead and when I stopped to check up and make notes he was well in the lead. His speed seemed to be between 50 and 55 miles per hour.

"At no time did the bird flap its wings, but sailed majestically along on an 'even keel'. The wind velocity was about 15 to 20 miles per hour on the ground, with a direction from east to west . . ."

Dead trees are favored for perching and roosting, and the birds are particularly partial to conifers. The big-cone spruce is a tall tree native to their habitat, and is a variety that appears to have existed

104

since the glacial period and is therefore known to condors through ages of association.

These roosting trees are usually from 40 to 70 feet high. The big-cone spruce is tall and has relatively few branches to obstruct take-offs and landings. It is apt to grow where air currents are regular and predictable. Given a choice, condors seem to prefer these trees to cliffs as roosting and perching places, because the air near cliffs is often turbulent and approach and exit directions are limited. Birds usually roost within three feet of the trunk of a tree, probably because branches are larger and more stable there. As many as half a dozen may roost in the same tree. Condors sometimes use their beaks as parrots do to assist in moving from one branch to another. Birds do roost on cliffs and regularly use cliff ledges to preen and sun themselves.

Cattle, especially calves, seem to be preferred above all other food, and condors like their meat quite fresh. Possibly in the days when sheep were plentiful in their range, condors preferred sheep as well. Modern baitings with sheep have often proved successful. At present, cattle, sheep, ground squirrels, deer, and horses furnish 95% of their food. Yet ten condors were observed feeding on one Angora cat. Fish, mussels, and skunks are also consumed. The condor has a generous appetite. His job is to consume and he does so. His remarkable constitution allows him to eat enough at one time to sustain him for up to a week. Thus when condors feed on squirrels, rabbits or other small game, an ample supply is usually present. The great birds do not usually waste effort in descending for one squirrel at a time. It would be as uneconomical as a big jet landing ten times en route from Chicago to New York.

Condors do strange things. A Santa Barbara hunter reports: "They paid little attention to me, and would have been easy prey for the Sunday .22. Earlier that afternoon a condor followed me for about forty-five minutes as I looked for boar signs. The country was hilly grassy country with clumps of oaks and small stands of pines. With a great whoosh of wings, the bird would swoop low over me, then land on the nearest tree, as if waiting for me to make a kill at whose remains it could feast. I could think of no other reason for its behavior. In the depth of the wilderness, it had probably learned to follow the big predators."

Captive condors will eat fresh meat and wild condors often feed on animals that have been dead only a few minutes. There is no record of them attacking live animals. The chief advantage to the condor waiting until a carcass has decayed a day or more is that the hide, if tough, is usually softened and thus more easily penetrated. The birds feed only during the day, and when feeding alone they are watchful, but when in groups they seem to become almost oblivious to their surroundings. Observers have approached to within a hundred yards of 17 condors feeding on the carcass of a horse, and numerous cases are recorded of men approaching, capturing, or killing the birds under similar circumstances.

Harry Harris, historian and author of *The Annals of Gymnogyps*, describes the feeding scene in the motion pictures taken by J.R. Pemberton:

"Such a scene has been recorded . . . in at least one section of the Pemberton film, which shows fourteen individuals devouring a coyote-killed sheep; the writer can vouch for the not entirely peaceful nature of the gathering. Two great old fellows had evidently selected the same spot for a landing and there had been a slight collision. They began immediately to box, dancing heavily and clumsily about, slapping at each other with upraised wings, the red of their wrinkled heads seemingly intensified in anger, and for the moment they were too engrossed in personal differences to have at the sheep, while the rest of the crowd with the utmost dispatch was filling up on mutton."

Condors share food with other birds. They will tolerate crows, ravens, turkey vultures and eagles on the same carcass. As many as 50 ravens, crows, vultures, in addition to numerous condors, have been seen circling over a carcass, and it is a memorable sight to see these gradations of dark birds assembled in the air or on the ground at a single feeding spot. Usually eagles will drive condors from a carcass, but the condor's quiet patience and group feeding habits may prevail over the more aggressive qualities of the eagles. Koford observed, beginning at 7 a.m., a condor land 100 feet from the carcass of a deer on which an eagle was feeding. The eagle flew at the condor and chased it 100 yards in the air before returning to the deer. The same action was repeated with another condor a few minutes later and with others throughout the morning. At 1:30 p.m., 16 condors landed 100 yards from the carcass, but took off when the eagle rushed at them. Yet ten minutes later 12 condors were on the ground, and were again driven away. At 2:30, 14 condors landed and were chased away. This time the pursuing eagle struck one of them with his talons but apparently caused no injury. Often the eagle did not come within 50 feet of the pursued birds. The condors twisted and dodged as they fled. At 3:30, 23 condors appeared and alighted nearby. Forty minutes later they had moved to within 20 yards of the carcass and did not leave when the eagle chased one or two away. Finally the eagle flew away and the flock moved in on the carcass.

William L. Dawson reported an even more dramatic and amusing example of group effort on the condor's part. An aggressive eagle had chased three condors from their perch on a tall dead pine. The condors departed to another tree a short distance higher on the ridge. There they appeared to take counsel. A few minutes later, a black winged bombshell struck the perched eagle and knocked him from his perch. Before he could recover and take punitive action, a second feathered bombshell struck him, this time in mid-air. The eagle changed his mind and left the area.

Feeding condors may be easily disturbed. People should not approach within half a mile so as not to disturb them as they eat. Often though, condors may appear to exhibit no alarm at all when humans are near. For example, they may not leave a perch in a tree under which a man has stood until he has walked a quarter mile or more away. The bird may peer down at the person occasionally, or merely seem to be preoccupied with preening and rearranging its feathers. This misleads many people into thinking that condors do not fear man and do not need privacy. Carl Koford made many observations of the reactions of a pair of nesting condors to disturbance and actual entrance of their nest site by humans. He states:

"Persons unacquainted with the psychology of birds frequently misinterpret actions . . . as indicating tameness in nesting condors. Rather, these actions are innate responses to extreme alarm. These responses are strongest during the brooding stage. Certain essential activities, such as feeding the chick, are not performed when the adults are in a state of alarm."

Many authorities feel condors are in little danger of starving. Though it is true that the immense herds of cattle, sheep and wild animals that once roamed their range have diminished, so have the condors diminished, and there are sufficient cattle and deer herds, especially, as well as squirrels and rabbits, to supply their feeding needs. However, it is also true that the disappearance of the great domestic livestock herds of the mission and rancho eras and of the period immediately following the Gold Rush removed a food supply that had helped maintain a larger condor population. Older methods of handling livestock which often allowed animals to die on the range and remain there produced more condor food than modern methods which tend to keep animals alive or dispose of carcasses. Droughts and forest fires have an effect on condor food supplies, but normally they are not drastic. Areas protected from burning become overgrown with heavy brush which hides carcasses and is unsuitable for the condor, with its large wingspread, to land. Fire consumes the overgrowth and may thus aid foraging. The present food supply is probably adequate, but since areas suitable for nesting may not have readily accessible food, a program of providing road-killed carcasses near known nesting sites has been carried out in recent years.

Condors have regular drinking and bathing places in secluded spots in the wild country. Their favorite pools have sandy banks and are not more than three or four inches deep. The water is always clear but not always running. These pools are in a high open location where the birds may land and take off with ease.

Condors drink shortly after feeding and often visit a pool on their way back from foraging. The daily bath is a regular procedure from March until cold weather comes in the fall. The protection and seclusion of these rare pools is essential to the welfare of the condors.

In another observation, Forest Service Assistant Supervisor C.S. Robinson reported witnessing a courting display. He saw "a large 'male' bird strutting around displaying his wings, similar to the action of domestic tom turkeys. This was near Big Pine Lookout in September 1936, on a ledge of rock a quarter mile away. The 'female' remained quietly sitting while the male strutted in semi-circles in front of her. He would perform exactly as a wild or domestic turkey—dragging his wings, etc. It was too far away to see closely even with field glasses, but I could note the erect carriage, with the head held first high and then lowered to the ground . . ."

Condors possibly mate for life and their courting, as Robinson noted, is similar to other birds'. The male faces its partner at a distance of three to six feet and spreads his wings, flashing the white coverts, and lowers his head. He begins to display by holding his wings out to the sides, inflating his neck, and probably hissing as the

Andean condor has been observed to do. He turns slowly from side to side, then walks back and forth in front of the female with short shuffling steps and may approach and retreat several times before mating occurs. Often the female appears unimpressed by the display, and more annoyed than submissive. When the male becomes persistent, she will peck or nibble at the back of his lowered head. Usually the birds fly off together after display.

The pair select the nest site together, and egg laying occurs in February and March.

At other times, pairs of condors have been observed in mutual display. They face each other with wings outspread to reveal the white underwing feathers, then cross necks, nuzzle and nibble each other about the head and beak. Usually they sit quietly side by side after doing this. It is likely a "pair bonding" mechanism as condors later found to have been caring for an egg or recently hatched chick were seen to exhibit this behavior.

Condors do not mate until they are at least six or seven years old. Some authorities suggest that the birds likely evolved to maintain reproductive vigor "well past half of a century." Pairs of condors have been known to remate and to use the same nests over a period of years.

Nests are usually holes or protected niches in cliff faces, though there is a record of condors nesting in a large hollow in a sequoia tree. Nests are not fabricated by the birds. They consist of the barest essentials, namely, a sheltered place for the egg to rest, usually the floor of a small cave or pothole containing a bit of sand or drifted leaves. There must be room for two adult condors, suitable roosting places nearby, and convenient perches for the young bird when it leaves the nest. Pairs of condors may use various nesting sites at different times; availability of food nearby possibly determines their choice.

Eggs are approximately 4½ inches long by 2½ inches in diameter, and the shell is pale green or blue. Incubation takes from 50 to 60 days and most eggs hatch in April or May. Condors normally lay a single egg in a season, but may lay a second egg if the first is broken. Nestings are usually two or more years apart, although successful yearly nesting by pairs of condors has been observed.

When hatched, the chick is covered with soft grey down. In three months, feathers appear, and by six months the feathers have completed their growth and the bird is out of the nest and able to fly a little. At eight to ten months the young bird is flying with the adults. Its head remains dark grey-green, gradually changing to a bright red-orange by the time the bird is five or six, and the eyes have changed from brown to brilliant clear red. The juvenile condor associates with the parent birds until it is almost two years old, accompanying them to feeding sites and still being fed occasionally by them. Not until birds are five to six years old are they fully matured and exhibiting the distinctive adult plumage pattern.

Chicks and young birds hiss and grunt when alarmed, and regurgitate when actively threatened. When deeply apprehensive for each other or for the safety of their chick, adult birds make a low whining sound like a dog or human.

Topatopa is the only California condor in captivity. She has resided in the Los Angeles Zoo, away from public view, since 1967. Estimated to be eight or nine months old when found, she was weak and hungry and apparently had been deserted by her parents. Perhaps her limited flying ability had brought her to earth in an area too close to human activity, and too brushy for the young bird to easily become airborne again. She obviously had not fed for a long time. An attempt was made to return her to the wild after zoo personnel had treated her and she had regained her strength. She was released in an area where it was hoped the parent birds would find her, but she was returned to the zoo after being observed at the release site for eight days. It became apparent that she could not be reunited with the adults and was still too young to survive on her own.

There are about forty condors in existence today. Probably more important than this estimated total population is the number of confirmed nestings. These have declined to one or two in recent years.

However, the condor is a remarkably persistent bird. Time and again experts have predicted death of this species. Yet condors fly today as in centuries past. If man can temper concern with caution, and offer protection, space and solitude for these giant birds, they may continue to soar over wild places during our own tenure on earth.

CONDOR
HABITAT
TODAY

CONSERVATION AND CONTROVERSY

In 1932 Dr. Alexander Wetmore of the Smithsonian Institution estimated there were 10 condors in existence. The following year 17 were seen in one flock, then 20, then more. The birds had fooled the experts. There were more than anyone had guessed.

The 1933-34 sightings received unexpected publicity. The condor had in effect been rediscovered. But a handful of cattlemen, sheepmen, hunters, fishermen, forest rangers and wilderness roamers had known all along the birds were there, were able to say I told you so.

It now seems incredible that such a bird should have "escaped" organized conservation efforts so long. Official interest in the modern condor may be said to date from 1933 when the Forest Service made its first organized attempt to determine the numbers of condors within the boundaries of Santa Barbara National Forest, now in the Los Padres National Forest. The Forest Service was in a sense the custodian of the birds since most remaining condor habitats were on national forest land.

Under direction of Forest Supervisor S.A. Nash-Boulden and with field work supervised by Assistant Supervisor C.S. Robinson, fire lookouts, patrolmen, and trail crews went to work for the condor. Forest Service records from 1909 to 1932 were a virtual blank, as far as the birds were concerned, and reflected the general apathy and hopelessness toward the condor's future. Now things were suddenly different. To quote from the milestone report by Robinson:

"In 1934 attention was focused on the upper Sisquoc River Drainage, where it was thought a colony was established around Mission Pine Mountain or the Hurricane Deck area. Condors were often seen in the Cuyama Valley and also near Soda Lake (Carrizo Plain). Bertram Snedden of the Snedden Ranch and Cattle Company told of their appearance occasionally at Salisbury and Santa Barbara Potreros and said that he and his riders had watched them feeding on dead cattle. Snedden also spoke of their appearance around San Emidgio Mt. and at Tejon Pass. Eugene Johnson, stockman in the Cuyama Valley, also reported birds in considerable quantity.

"At the end of 1934 Los Padres officers estimated the numbers of condors on the Forest to be about 60 birds and were in a position to plan more intensive observation for the following year. It was difficult to get information as the Forest officers were widely scattered. However, in 1935, the concentration points—two main roosts or gathering grounds—were located. The largest was near the Sisquoc Falls in Santa Barbara County; the other in the Whiteacre Peak-Hopper Mountain Creek area in Ventura County. At the close of the year the numbers of California Condor, within the counties of Santa Barbara and Ventura, were placed at between 50 and 60 . . ."

"The year 1936 afforded the first opportunity to make some really worthwhile studies and plans for the future. Arrangements were made to place a competent man at each concentration point for a

30-day period. These men were members of the summer fire patrol force, normally on duty in June, but to go on duty a month earlier. Their instructions were simple—to record carefully from daylight to dark the numbers of condors seen, together with the date, time and place. By this method it was felt an accurate count could be obtained. If observer A on May 10 at 3:00 p.m. counted 18 condors in the air, and observer B, 25 miles distant, counted 15 birds at the same hour, a total of 33 was assured. Supplementary notes on direction of flight, characteristic markings and similar observations were also recorded.

"Unfortunately money for such a project again was not available so it was necessary to plan how this essential information could be obtained by using regular men during the summer months. About that time John Baker, of the National Association of Audubon Societies, who was particularly interested in the California Condor, called at the Supervisor's office in April. The problem was discussed and Baker was able to obtain contributions from members in southern California to pay the wages of our observers. The two men, Jake Johns and Walter Maples, were placed accordingly; Johns at Whiteacre Peak and Maples at the Sisquoc Falls. Field headquarters were located nearby; supplies were packed in; and both men were on the job May 5, 1936. The following memorandum for files of April 17, 1936, written by Mr. Nash-Boulden, Forest Supervisor, gives a good outline of the situation."

113

After going over our maps showing possible range covered, probable nesting places, and colonies of birds, etc., field trips were planned. The main objectives of the trips were to acquaint Baker with the Forest area and habitat of the California Condor; and to give Baker a view of the birds and where they can usually be found; also to discuss the effect of disturbance by people or roads. Many other matters concerning their life habits, numbers, feeding, bathing, nesting, etc., were also taken up.

The first trip was from Santa Barbara to the Salisbury Potero on the Cuyama District. We were able to sketch out on the ground the present impossibility of affording adequate protection to the Upper Sisquoc River watershed in the case of fire. Difficulties in alternate routes for the road were discussed and the necessity of major-divide roads pointed out. The matter of possible disturbance of the birds by such a road and problems of additional closure to public use was also discussed.

At this time Supervisor Nash-Boulden agreed with Baker that the construction of the Hurricane Deck Road would be pushed on only so as to connect with a good spring—a possible distance of about 1½ miles. Further road construction on into the Sisquoc River was to be held up pending a thorough survey by the U.S. Forest Service of the conditions around the Upper Sisquoc River with special reference to possible nesting and bathing places of the California Condor at the Sisquoc Falls.

The second trip was to the Whiteacre Peak country and we were able to see several condors in the air in the vicinity of the peak and Hopper Mountain Creek. Two mature birds were observed with field glasses as well as one young bird. The young bird was a darker color and white underwing feathers were not distinct, nor was there the characteristic orange-colored wattling. The feet were a dark gray as opposed to the yellow-colored feet of the mature birds. Three more birds were seen far off, making a total of six seen April 15."

Robinson's report continues with evidence that animal predators may occasionally kill condors. "Coyotes, bobcats, and cougars may kill condors when they find them at a fresh kill. These predators are known to return to their kills and condor feathers have been found near such locations. It would be comparatively easy to attack the condors, when gorged to such an extent flight from the ground is difficult . . .

"Storms may also be a possible factor in accidental death. This has been overlooked, as shown by the following quite accurate report in the *Los Angeles Times,* October 25, 1936. This gives an account of finding two dead condors by Forest Officers.

The mysterious deaths of two of a colony of three American condors

114

in Peach Tree Flat region of Los Padres National Forest was cleared today after a post mortem conducted by Ornithologist Egmont Z. Rett of the Museum of Natural History in Mission Canyon.

The loss of two of the small remaining colony of the largest birds that fly over America is definitely laid at the door of a hail storm.

The mountain tragedy was discovered by Sam Kosub, Forest Service foreman, at Sunset Valley Camp, where he was sent into the Peach Tree country with several CCC boys to look for lightning fires. They came across the carcass of a horse and nearby a dead condor, while a second bird lay some distance away. A third condor, apparently badly injured, flew away. Hail still lay piled in surrounding gullies to a depth of from two to three feet, some of the hailstones as large as walnuts.

Post mortem by Rett showed that the backs of both birds were broken. Foresters believe the condors came to feed on the carcass of the horse. In all probability the birds were stunned by the terrific force of hail when in flight and fell to the ground from a considerable height.

"Both of these birds were mounted by Rett and preserved—one is at the Museum and the other at the U.S. Forest Service headquarters in Santa Barbara . . ."

In 1963, the Forest Service offered their bird to the Santa Barbara Museum of Natural History where it may now be seen in a permanent habitat display.

Pools of liquid petroleum proved fatal to ancient condors and are still a menace to the birds, Robinson's findings indicate.

"Old residents of Maricopa said that about 1918 the condors were often seen on the plains east of town and farther north around McKittrick where sheep grazed. They also spoke of several birds that had lit near large oil pools, believing them to be water, and had become fouled with oil and later picked up dead. In recent years the pools have dried up, or have been diverted into tanks, reducing this hazard. However no condors have been seen there in recent years, except in flight.

"Shooting undoubtedly is responsible for the highest man-caused loss. Undoubtedly, stupid people have killed many of the birds in the past. Cowboys from some of the large cattle ranches have told of their predecessors who shot the birds 'just for the target practice' . . . Deer hunters in the past have killed them and may still do so, but this is at least considerably reduced. There are, however, very many opportunities for promiscuous shooting, as the condor in the air offers an unusual and perhaps easy target. Recently a 'sportsman' said he thought the bird was an eagle and promptly shot it, in spite of the fact that eagles are fully protected by State laws ..."

And finally Robinson concluded: "According to the Los Padres annual report, the total number of condors resident on this Forest was estimated on December 31, 1938 at between 55 and 60. We are fairly safe in giving this number and also estimating that of this total there are about ten immature birds varying from one to three years old ... Shooting and egg stealing are now perhaps the greatest risks, with disturbance always a serious contributing factor."

Robinson's report summarized the first extensive field studies ever made of the condor in modern terms. It helped initiate a whole series of events whose end is not yet in sight.

As a beginning the Forest Service abandoned plans for a fire protection road leading from the Manzana Creek over Hurricane Deck and up the Sisquoc River. The road would have penetrated the last wilderness remaining in that section of Los Padres Forest and would have gone through the heart of condor country. The Forest Service then joined with the National Audubon Society, local groups and individuals in establishing the Sisquoc Condor Sanctuary in 1937. Some 1,200 acres near the headwaters of the Sisquoc River were set aside as the first decisive step by man toward recognition and preservation of the condor.

No sooner had the Sisquoc Sanctuary been established than many birds left the area. Their departure coincided with road-building activities within their immediate flight and roosting range, and most experts agree there was a direct connection between these activities and the departure of the birds.

Next, the Forest Service, backed by conservationists and many local and national groups, closed a large area in the lower Sespe region of Ventura County to the public. This area was established as the Sespe Wildlife Preserve in 1947. The Forest Service provided a special condor patrolman as guard, and for several years the National Audubon Society provided funds to pay approximately half of his salary.

Today the Audubon Society provides the full-time services of a Condor Naturalist, John C. Borneman, for educational and field study programs.

The discovery of oil nearby soon brought pressure on the newest sanctuary. Its oil and mineral deposits were under control of the

Department of the Interior, not of the Department of Agriculture—the Forest Service's parent department—and a series of hearings followed best described as red hot.

In 1951, the Secretary of the Interior issued an order stating that 55 square miles of land in the Los Padres Forest were to be "withdrawn from all forms of appropriation under the public-land laws, including the mining laws," and "with certain exceptions, the mineral leasing laws, and reserved as a condor sanctuary, under the jurisdiction of the Forest Service."

In the 16 square miles where nesting and roosting were concentrated, there was to be no public entry to the surface of the ground, though oil and gas could be tapped by directional drilling from outside the area.

Within the remaining 39 square miles, oil, gas, and mineral deposits could be developed, provided that no one in so doing approached within half a mile of a condor nest active within three years.

Many persons opposed these conservation measures, feeling withdrawal of such an area from public surface use was too great a sacrifice of the public domain for the sake of a doomed bird.

A similar view was held by stockmen who wished to graze cattle in the closed portion of the sanctuary.

Areas important to condor survival were placed under further moratorium in the early 1970s by both the Department of the Interior and the Bureau of Land Management.

But the controversies continued, the sanctuary still under pressure from private and "public" interests, and the birds continued to fly, while conservationists battled each threat to the condors and their last refuge.

Carl Koford, a leading authority on the California condor, pointed out that lack of interest and apathy of those in a position to take action were the major obstacles to attempts to save the bird during the 1940s and 50s. He also pointed out that the bird's chief enemy continues to be man. His study report, *The California Condor*, published in 1953, stated: "A condor seems to be a tempting target for a man or boy with a gun. Cooper (1890) . . . and Stephens (1919) gave shooting as one of the main reasons for the decrease of the numbers of condors. E.T. Mendenhall and J.B. Dixon of San Diego County told me that in the late 1800s it was the ambition of every boy to shoot a

117

condor. W. Lee Chambers had a sporting goods store near Santa Monica from 1896 to 1905. At that time the first high-powered sporting rifles came into use and there was much indiscriminate shooting. Two condors which had been shot were brought into Chamber's store about 1905.

"In 1925, the San Diego Natural History Museum was given a freshly mounted condor by an anonymous party with a stipulation that no questions be asked. In 1927, a hunter drove into Santa Barbara with a condor, which he had shot, tied to his car . . . In 1929, a young condor, shot through the wing, was found near Fillmore. This bird survived for ten years at the San Diego Zoo. About 1932, a condor which had been shot was found near Lebec by Harold Bowhay of Bakersfield. The bird died in captivity.

"In 1944, a rancher flushed a large group of condors near Porterville. One struck a wire fence and was injured. The rancher shot it and the specimen was mounted. Another rancher admitted to me that a few years ago he shot several times at a large bird in the belief it was a golden eagle before he saw it was a condor. A sheep rancher, who killed two golden eagles in San Luis Obispo County about 1946, said he would shoot any condors which he saw near his sheep. He refused to be convinced that condors were not predatory.

"It is not impossible that, on the average, at least one condor is shot each year. There are several thousand hunters on some ranger districts on the Los Padres National Forest in the first week of the deer hunting season. Many of these hunters are from distant areas and they have not heard of condors.

Condors undoubtedly continue to be shot, although few instances are authenticated. During their field studies for the National Audubon Society, National Geographic Society, and University of California condor report, the McMillan brothers compiled reports of people shooting at condors. At least two birds were said to have been killed in 1963. In May 1964 one of the study team saw a ranch worker shoot at a condor near Arvin in Kern County. The bird appeared to have been hit. One leg was dangling loosely as it flew away. The incident was reported and the man arrested. He testified that he had shot at a buzzard. In spite of the fact that turkey vultures are also protected, the man was acquitted.

California law fully protects the condor as a nongame bird and endangered species. Condors and their eggs were exempted from scientific collection for many years. However in 1952, permission was given the San Diego Zoo by the State Fish and Game Commission to trap a pair of condors for scientific purposes. This trapping attempt had its humorous side. When the trapper went into the backcountry, nature and the birds seemed to conspire against him. Rain and snow hampered his operations and the birds refused to be trapped. Meanwhile public indignation was rising. Strong protest developed and the State Legislature passed a resolution directing the Fish and Game Commission to issue no more condor-trapping permits. The effect of this resolution was later incorporated into the State Fish and Game Code. However in 1971 the code was amended and it again became possible to issue permits for collecting fully protected species, including the condor, for scientific purposes.

The code continues to provide a fine of $1,000 and/or one year in jail for taking a condor, but at the time of this writing only one person is known to have been punished for condor killing. He shot one near Pasadena in 1908, attempted to sell it and was fined $50 under an 1880s statute.

In September, 1976, an injured condor was discovered by two hunters near Grapevine in Kern County. They notified a State Fish and Game warden who captured the bird. It was taken to the Los Angeles Zoo and examined by veterinarians. They determined that the bird had been shot approximately two weeks earlier. X-rays of the shattered wing showed lead fragments in the area of the break. The condor was weak, emaciated, and weighed only about twelve pounds. Antibiotic treatment was begun to arrest the infection. It was decided that surgical repair would be attempted when the condor had regained weight and recovered from shock. By the end of October, it was much improved; a team of four veterinarians operated on the injured wing. They were forced to amputate it. The bird died two days later.

Federal protection began in 1942 when the Convention on Nature Protection and Wildlife Preservation in the Western Hemisphere, otherwise known as the Natural Resources Treaty, became effective. Unfortunately, no federal laws were passed to implement the convention but it had the effect of calling attention to the issue and giving the condor national recognition. The 1949 International Technical Conference on the Protection of Nature at Lake Success included the California condor among thirteen birds of the world "in need of emergency action if they are to be saved from extinction." Thus the United Nations recognized the condor as a threatened species. In 1966, the passage of the Endangered Species Preservation Act directed the Secretary of the Interior to develop a list of endangered species. The California condor was included in this first official register published in 1967. Finally the Endangered Species Act passed by Congress in 1973 made the taking of any endangered species a violation of federal law.

Earlier, in 1965, at the direction of Congress the Endangered Wildlife Research Program was initiated at Patuxent Wildlife Research Center, Maryland, by the U.S. Fish and Wildlife Service. A professional biologist, Fred C. Sibley, was assigned to full-time research on the California condor, a position currently held by Sanford R. Wilbur. Also in 1965 the first annual Condor Survey was begun. Expert observers were stationed at strategic points in the condor range. Their sightings were correlated to provide an estimate of each year's population in terms of numbers, age, and general welfare. Results showed a steady decline in numbers. By 1976 the total condor population was estimated at forty birds. Equally significant was the declining reproduction rate. No more than two young per season had been hatched in recent years. But an estimated four to six young birds must be produced annually and survive to breed if the present population is to be maintained.

The Condor Recovery Team, originally formed in 1965 as the Condor Survey Committee to act as technical advisors in research and management, coordinates the efforts of various agencies concerned with condor survival. Representatives from the Fish and Wildlife Service, Bureau of Land Management, Forest Service, California Department of Fish and Game, and the National Audubon Society are appointed to the team by the Director of the Fish and Wildlife Service under provisions of the Endangered Species Act. A comprehensive management guide aimed at restoring the condor to a population of fifty birds was adopted in 1975 as the Condor Recovery Plan. Under this program, supplemental feeding programs are carried out in an attempt to encourage nesting. Carcasses of deer killed on roads by automobiles are placed in foraging areas near known nesting sites in hopes that an adequate and readily available food supply may encourage the birds to breed. Results so far are inconclusive. In addition, five Critical Habitat Areas have been established within the condor range. They cover major nesting, roosting, and foraging sites. Within those portions of these areas that lie on federal lands, primary consideration must be given to the protection of the condor. This does not mean the birds are being locked up or hidden from public view. Officially designated points at Dough Flat and Mt. Pinos in the Los Padres National Forest make it possible for people to see condors without disturbing their nests or roosts.

The Endangered Species Act provides that allocations from the Land and Water Conservation Fund can be used to acquire additional habitat for endangered species. The Condor Recovery Plan proposed additional land acquisition and by 1976 more than 2,500 acres considered vital to the survival of the condor had been added. These included the 162 acre Huff's Hole property in San Luis Obispo County, the 320 acre Green Cabins parcels and the 58 acre Coldwater Canyon tract, both private inholdings within the Sespe Condor Sanctuary, and the 1,800 acre Hopper Mountain National Wildlife Refuge. National Audubon Society, The Nature Conservancy, together with the Forest Service, Fish and Wildlife Service, and the California Dept. of Fish and Game are cooperating on these acquisition projects and negotiations continue for further expanding habitat area. They are also concerned with protection of air space above condor habitats. California law already prohibits aircraft from flying lower than 3,000 feet over condor sanctuaries.

If supportive and protective measures aimed at arresting the condor's decline prove inadequate, the Recovery Team is charged with the responsibility for providing a Contingency Plan. This may involve a more drastic approach to condor preservation than anything yet tried. Recovery Team agencies are evaluating a captive breeding proposal that has already sparked a growing controversy.

Conflicts over proper methods of condor management have arisen for many years. When a commercial photographer was allowed into the Sespe Condor Sanctuary with Forest Service approval and assistance, the Audubon Society and the Forest Service, traditionally partners in condor preservation, were suddenly on opposite sides.

They were again in conflict when the Forest Service proposed to complete and open for public use as a motorized through-way an existing fire-protection road along the Sierra Madre Ridge, an ancient condor flyway within a few miles of the Sisquoc Sanctuary. Local citizens and conservation groups became involved. The road was eventually completed but not surfaced as originally proposed, and was closed to public use where it most closely approached the sanctuary. Continuing efforts of local and national groups resulted in the closure of an additional five miles of the controversial road.

In the mid-1960s the Sespe Sanctuary was once again threatened, this time on more massive scale. A $90 million dam and recreational project was proposed for Sespe Canyon in the heart of condor country. An access road would have cut through the sanctuary. Proponents of the project made the now familiar arguments: it would control floods, provide jobs and recreational opportunities, enhance underground irrigational water supplies, and some of them grumbled that "forty dirty birds—flying garbage cans" shouldn't be allowed to stand in the way of "progress." Alarmed conservationists, aware of the harmful impact the dam would have on one of the birds' last retreats, joined forces with other citizens who saw the project as a costly tax burden. Emotion ran high. The developers formed their own group of ornithological experts who proposed to save the birds with feeding and capture programs. The turning point came when E.D. Marshall, a practical minded condor preservationist and former Forest Service official, was able to show convincingly that the dam project would touch many people's pocketbooks adversely. The required bond issue was defeated by a margin of 40 votes out of a total of nearly 15,000.

But the issue is not settled. In 1970 the Secretary of the Interior felt obliged to oppose a revived Sespe Water Project because of the detrimental effects it might have on the condor, and again in the spring of 1977 the matter was presented to the Ventura Board of Supervisors. So the struggles continue.

If condors were content to stay inside their two sanctuaries, perhaps their chances of survival would be assured. But they persist in living as condors have always lived, ranging for miles to forage on private and public land, roosting and nesting in places of their own choosing, flying now and then to inspect the city limits of Santa Barbara or San Jose. The result is constant conflict with man's expanding use of his environment and resources.

When a large corporation proposed strip mining for phosphates in a portion of the Los Padres National Forest dangerously close to the Condor Critical Habitat Area buffering the Sespe Sanctuary, the friends of the condor found themselves battling once again to protect wild places and wild bird. The condor had become a symbol in the critical relationship between man and nature. The bird is like the canary in the coal mine. If he languishes, can the environment be healthy for other living creatures including man?

Soon the ultimate decisions must be made. But so far no phosphate has been mined at the proposed site on the slopes of Pine Mountain.

Meanwhile opinion is sharply divided within the conservation community as to the merits of the Condor Recovery Team's Contingency Plan to capture condors and attempt a breeding program. Proponents of this admittedly last-ditch effort cite the success of the Andean condor breeding program at the San Diego Zoo where 11 birds have been reared in nine years. Removal of the first egg for incubation has induced the Andean birds to produce a second in the same season. It is hoped that California condors may also breed in captivity and birds could be returned to the wild population. Weighing heavily against this hope, however, is the fact that no captive-bred Andean condors have been reintroduced into a wild environment.

Opponents of the captive breeding plan agree that the decline of the condor is indeed alarming. They also believe that implementing such a plan will hasten the extinction of the species. Capture attempt will, they argue, risk broken bones and traumatic injury to the birds. Furthermore, it is impossible to determine the sex of a condor without sophisticated laboratory testing of blood, fecal matter, or feather pulp. Cloacal examination in the field may be an alternative. In the first procedure, captured birds would be confined until test results were completed. In the second, internal examination under field conditions would be difficult and dangerous. Meaningful testing of hormone levels seems to require that the birds be in the breeding cycle, and cloacal evidence of sex may be visible only at that time. The effects of handling or of even brief confinement are unknown.

Inadvertent capture of immatures or other nontarget birds, plus the possibility that a large number of condors would have to be taken and examined to achieve the desired sex ratio, could well place a fatal stress on a species already known for its inability to tolerate intrusion of its environment, let alone such manhandling. Nesting birds might be captured. So might birds still engaged in feeding a nestling or an immature from the previous year. Young birds apparently depend on their parents for part of their sustenance until they are almost two years old. This long associative period is also probably one of learning to forage and cope with their environment. How this vital training stage can be artificially provided for birds reared in captivity is not clear.

Assuming birds are captured, will they breed? Since the trigger mechanisms for the California condor's breeding cycle are unknown, it is by no means certain that the captives would breed successfully in their new situation, despite the fact that Andean condors have done so.

Even if young are produced, will it be possible to release them successfully into a wild environment? Topatopa, the female condor now in the Los Angeles Zoo, was about nine months old when found, fully fledged and able to fly for short distances. After she had been treated at the zoo for eleven days, she was released into a wild environment but when it became obvious that she could not survive without her parents, she was returned to the zoo. And if chicks are successfully reared and released, will they have the immunity to resist diseases and parasites present in the wild population?

The Condor Recovery Team is fully aware of these and other risks involved. Capture will be made in areas where condors forage and roost, rather than near the known nesting sites, in an effort to avoid interference. Captive-raised young condors would not be freed until they are from five to ten years old and fully matured. Facilities for the breeding program must be provided away from zoo populations, and in areas relatively free from air pollution. Methods used to success- fully release peregrine falcons to the wild can possibly be adapted for reintroducing condors to a wild environment. Peregrine falcons must learn to kill in order to survive. Condors may only need to be provided with carrion until they are able to find their own food.

The Contingency Plan calls for the initial capture of at least three condors, one female and two males. Topatopa, the female already in captivity, would be the fourth member, making two pairs to be used in the first breeding attempts. The following year, the capture of two more pairs is proposed, and if the program appears to be working well, another two pairs might be taken the succeeding year.

As yet, this Contingency Plan has not been endorsed by all agencies and organizations involved with condor management. Should they do so, groups and individuals will be able to review the details of the plan and make comments and suggestions before any final decisions are made.

Looking to the future, can we expect man's efforts at condor

124

management, unsuccessful so far, will be any more successful with birds raised in captivity released into a shrinking wild environment where pollution threatens most forms of life? We know that the shells of condors' eggs show structural changes and thinning. This DDT effect is well known and has brought many bird species close to extinction. In the years since World War II millions of tons of toxic pesticides, herbicides, rodent control compounds, and agricultural chemicals have entered the food chains and the environment. Many of these have been found in the bodies of dead condors. Hormone levels affecting reproduction may be disrupted by concentrations of some of these chemical compounds. An alarming increase of mercury, lead, zinc, and other metals concentrated in condor feathers has occurred within the last ten years. Is man destroying the life around him? Isn't it time to stop and ask ourselves what we are really doing? The condor needs no more than any other living thing: clean air to breathe, freedom from molestation, room to live.

In the Condor Survey of October 1976, five flying immature birds from previous years were identified among the forty condors in the estimated count. Two fledglings were discovered later in the year. By August 1977, the parents of one of these were found to be caring for a second fledgling in the same nest. The theory that condors produce young no more often than every other year should be re-examined in the light of the documented activities of this pair, as well as the condors in the Hi Mountain area of San Luis Obispo County that are known to have successfully reared young four consecutive years in the 1960s. Historical accounts of yearly nesting should be re-evaluated. Given the right circumstances, condors may be capable of greater nesting success than we have assumed. Many authorities point out that lack of information on vital aspects of condor biology and behavior raises serious questions about the wisdom of drastic measures until more is learned and understood.

There may be more condors than official records indicate. Unconfirmed sightings continue to be reported from Baja California where condors ranged as late as the 1930s. From five to twelve birds have been claimed from this area in recent years. A joint U.S.-Mexican survey, in progress during 1977 in the Sierra San Pedro Mártir and Sierra Juarez, has been inconclusive, but this wild, remote region may still shelter condors following age-old survival instincts.

But we dare not become complacent. We need more than laws and government agencies. An educated public remains the most important element in any approach to the preservation of wildlife and wilderness. Traditionally, concerned individuals and citizen groups have led the way and are the ones who keep a watchful eye on the management of our wilderness heritage.

The condor symbolizes man's current troubled relationship with wild nature. In the words of one among many concerned with this problem, "If we cannot save the California condor and what he stands for, do we have the intelligence to save ourselves?"

This section of the San Rafael Mountains is a favorite condor flyway today.

Acknowledgments

The California condor has been part of my life for almost twenty years but I confess the plight of the bird was not the consuming interest for me that it came to be for Dick. When this expanded version of Dick Smith's *Condor Journal* was proposed, I offered to help. I knew he and our long-time friend, Noel Young, editor of Capra Press, were planning a new condor book based on Dick's recent work, the material was at hand and it seemed a fairly simple matter to correct and add to the original text of *California Condor: Vanishing American,* the book he co-authored with Robert Easton in 1964, and to help select from recent photographs and field notes.

Dick had this book in mind. Two weeks, he said, was all he needed to put it down on paper. But as I began to sort through his files, his hastily scribbled notebooks and stacks of photographs and slides, to listen to his excited voice on tape recordings as he watched condors soaring above him, and as I read through correspondence on wilderness and condors, the realization grew that this must be more than a collection of facts and pictures. There was emotion and caring in this material, the concern of many years. I hope I have been a faithful editor. I know I have come to value those who, officially or unofficially, also labor to save this valiant species and its last retreats. Without the help of even those who may have disagreed with Dick, this book could not have been written.

Dick's fellow trustees of the Santa Barbara Museum of Natural History and director, Dennis M. Power, established the "Dick Smith Memorial Fund" to co-publish this book with Capra Press. Staff members assisted with research and editing. Janet A. Hamber, Associate Curator of Vertebrate Zoology and a 1976 museum member of the Coast Range Population Condor Survey party, was indispensable as she shared personal observations and field notes, and literally guided me through vast amounts of file material necessary to correct and amend the original text. Her continuing studies and new discoveries add a hopeful epilogue to Dick's unfinished journal. D. Travis Hudson, Curator of Anthropology, made new information available from *Crystals in the Sky,* his own manuscript in progress, and helped to bring fresh insight to native North American historical and religious interaction with the California condor.

Clifton F. Smith, Curator of Botany and Museum Librarian,

identified photographs of condor habitat areas. Both he and Jan Timbrook, Assistant Curator of Anthropology, provided information to correct and amplify original material. The contribution of Waldo Abbott, Curator of Vertebrate Zoology (Retired), to the Smith/Easton manuscript carries over to this work.

Robert Easton, co-author of *California Condor: Vanishing American,* Dick's friend and trail companion, trusted me with a text as much his own as it was Dick's. He helped to rewrite and to organize the changes and additions for the years since their book was originally published.

One of the first to offer encouragement and suggestions was Sanford R. Wilbur, U.S. Fish and Wildlife Service Biologist, leader of the Condor Recovery Team. He provided me with reference material, concise listings of state and federal laws and regulations and the historical development and progress of condor management programs.

This journal also reflects field work and observations of many U.S. Forest Service personnel. Los Padres National Forest Supervisor Allan J. West and the staff co-operate in the Coast Range Population Condor Survey, providing assistance and trained observers. Monty Montagne, USFS Biologist, has been especially helpful. He and Dick traveled wilderness trails and studied the condor together for years. Monty's shared knowledge and reminiscences brought dimension to Dick's sometimes sketchy field notes.

John Borneman, Audubon Condor Naturalist, explained the background and preparation for the controversial Contingency Plan, aiding what I hope is a fair presentation of a program Dick opposed.

Christine Bent, Sybil Schutt, museum volunteers Alice Kladnick and Bette Eliason transcribed field notes and tapes, providing a workable typescript of the bits and pieces from which *Condor Journal* is drawn. Marie Ensign, Westmont College Library, contributed to the bibliographical material. Dr. Margaret Gott, museum volunteer, prepared the index. Ann Van Tyne, Santa Barbara Sierra Club, Joy Parkinson, Santa Barbara Audubon Society, so many knowledgeable people helped me in so many ways. I am grateful to them all.

The support and very real contributions of our children, Susan Soria, Judy Smith, Joel Smith, and Maren Jameson have been invaluable. From early childhood they explored the Santa Barbara coast and mountains with their father. If these pages reflect the essence of Dick's love of nature and his respect for life in all its forms, it is in part through their memories of him and the values he shared with them. Joel, who was a seasoned condor observer by his early teens, was especially helpful. He and his father had talked of condors and discussed new management proposals just days before Dick's death. Susan redrew Dick's maps from the original book to show changes and current information on the condor.

We thank all whose contributions to the Santa Barbara Museum's "Dick Smith Memorial Fund" have made the publication of Dick's work possible and will insure the continuation of the condor study he helped to establish.

—OLIVE KINGSTON SMITH

PRODUCTION CREDITS

Display and text typeset in Trump Mediaeval by Camera-ready Composition.
Cover design by Marcia Burtt.
Layout and pasteup by Christine Bent.
Maps by Susan Soria.
Camera and presswork by Haagen Printing in Santa Barbara.
Binding by Aaron Young.

BIBLIOGRAPHY

Audubon, J.J. 1840. *The Birds of America.* Vol. 1, p. 12-14. Philadelphia, J.B. Chevalier.

Audubon, J.W. 1906. *Audubon's Western Journal,* 1849-1850. Cleveland, Arthur H. Clark.

Bolton, H.E. 1927. *Fray Juan Crespí, Missionary Explorer on the Pacific Coast,* 1769-1774. Berkeley, University of California Press.

Borneman, J.C. 1966. "Return of a Condor." Audubon Magazine 68(3):154-157.

Boscana, G. 1933. *Chinigchinich,* Alfred Robinson's translation of Father Geronimo Boscana's historical account of the belief, usages, customs and extravagancies of the Indians of this Mission of San Juan Capistrano called the Acagchemem Tribe. Santa Ana, Fine Arts Press.

Brown, H. 1899. "The California Vulture in Arizona." Auk 16(3):272.

Bryant, W.E. 1891. "Andrew Jackson Grayson." Zoe 2(1):34-68.

California Condor Recovery Team. 1974. *California Condor Recovery Plan.* U.S. Fish and Wildlife Service.

California Department of Fish and Game. 1963. *California Department of Fish and Game Code,* Forty-third Edition. Sacramento.

Caras, R.A. 1970. *Source of the Thunder.* The biography of a California condor. Boston, Little, Brown and Co.

Clyman, J. 1926. "James Clyman, His Diaries and Reminiscences." California Historical Society Quarterly 6(2):136-137.

—— 1928. *James Clyman American Frontiersman 1792-1881.* Ed. C.L. Camp. California Historical Society Special Publication No. 3:1-251.

Dawson, W.L. 1923. *The Birds of California.* San Diego, South Moulton Co.

Dixon, J. 1924. "California condors breed in captivity." Condor 26(5):192.

Dyer, E.I. 1935. "Meeting the condor on its own ground." Condor 37(1):5-11.

Finley, W.L. 1906. "Life history of the California condor." Part I. Condor 8(6):135-142.

—— 1908a. "Life history of the California condor." Part II. Condor 10(1):5-10.

—— 1908b. "Life history of the California condor." Part III. Condor 10(2):59-65.

—— 1909. "General, a pet California condor." Country Life 16(1):35-38.

Fry, W. 1928. *The California Condor—A Modern Roc.* Sequoia National Park, Nature Guide Service, Bulletin 23.

Gass, P. 1904. *Gass' Journal of the Lewis and Clark Expedition.* Reprint of edition of 1811. Chicago, A.C. McClurg and Co.

Gifford, E.W. 1955. "Central Miwok Ceremonies." University of California Anthropological Records 14(4):261-317.

Harris, H. 1941. "The annals of *Gymnogyps* to 1900." Condor 43(1):3-55.

Howard, H. 1962. *Fossil Birds.* Los Angeles County Museum Science Series No. 17, Paleontology No. 10.

Howard, H. and A.H. Miller. 1939. "The avifauna associated with human remains at Rancho La Brea, California." Carnegie Institution of Washington Publication 514:39-48.

Hudson, T. and E. Underhay. No date. *Crystals in the Sky: an Odyssey into Chumash Astronomy, Cosmology and Rock Art.* Ballena Anthropological Papers, ed. by L. Bean and T. Blackburn. Socorro, Ballena Press (in press).

130

Koford, C.B. 1953. *The California Condor.* National Audubon Society Research Report 4.

Kroeber, A.L. 1906-07. "Indian myths of south central California." University of California Publication American Archaeology and Ethnology 4(4):167-250.

────── 1925. *Handbook of the Indians of California.* Smithsonian Institution Bureau of American Ethnology Bulletin 78.

Lewis, M. and W. Clark. 1809. *Travels of Capts. Lewis and Clarke.* London, Longman, Hurst, et al.

Loeb, E. 1926. "Pomo Folkways." University of California Publications American Archaeology and Ethnology 19(2):384-385.

Lucia, E. 1968. "Russian trek taps major history find." The Sacramento Bee. 22 September.

Mallette, R.D. 1971. "Results of California condor baiting effort, 1967-1969." California Department Fish and Game, Wildlife Management Branch Administrative Report 71-6.

McMillan, I. 1968. *Man and the California Condor.* New York, Dutton and Co.

Mertz, D.B. 1971. "The mathematical demography of the California condor population." American Naturalist 105(945):437-453.

Miller, A.H., I. McMillan and E. McMillan. 1965. *The Current Status and Welfare of the California Condor.* National Audubon Society Research Report 6.

Reddington, A.P. 1899. "Taking a condor's egg." Bulletin Cooper Ornithological Club 1(4):75.

Rett, E.Z. 1938. "Hailstorm fatal to California condors." Condor 40(5):225.

Richardson, W. 1969. "The wilderness that survived." Sage Magazine, Winter. Las Vegas, E.G. & G., Inc.

Rising, H. 1899. "Capture of a California condor." Condor 1(2):25-26.

Robinson, C.S. 1940. "Notes on the California condor, collected on Los Padres National Forest, California." U.S. Forest Service.

Scott, C.D. 1936. "Who killed the condor?" Nature Magazine 28(6):368-370.

Sibley, F.C. 1969. "Effects of the Sespe Creek Project on the California condor." U.S. Fish and Wildlife Service. Laurel, Maryland.

Sollen, R. 1977. "Metal intake afflicting condors?" Santa Barbara News-Press. 26 March:A-3.

Steufferud, A. (Ed.). 1966. *Birds in our lives.* U.S. Department of the Interior.

Stock, C. 1958. *Rancho La Brea.* Los Angeles County Museum Science Series No. 20. Paleontology No. 11.

Sumner, L. 1950. "Condors observed from an airplane." Condor 52(3):133.

Wetmore, A. 1959. "Birds of the Pleistocene in North America." Smithsonian Miscellaneous Collection 138(4):1-24.

Wilbur, S.R. 1972. "The food resources of the California condor." Fish and Wildlife Service, Patuxent Wildlife Research Center.

────── 1975. "California condor plumage and molt as field study aids." California Fish and Game 61(3):144-148.

────── 1976. "Condor: a doomed species?" National Parks and Conservation Magazine 50:15-19.

────── 1976. "Status of the California condor, 1972-1975." American Birds 30(4):789-790.

Wilbur, S.R., W.D. Carrier, J.C. Borneman and R.D. Mallette. 1972. "Distribution and numbers of the California condor, 1966-1971." American Birds 26(5):819-823.

Wilbur, S.R., W.D. Carrier and J.C. Borneman. 1974. "Supplemental feeding program for California condors." Journal of Wildlife Management 38(2):343-346.

Verner, J. 1976. "An appraisal of the continued involvement of Forest Service Research in the California condor recovery program." U.S. Forest Service, Pacific Southwest Forest and Range Experiment Station.

Suggested Reading

Advisory Committee on Predator Control. 1972. "Predator control—1971." Report to the Council on Environmental Quality and the Department of the Interior.

Aldington, R. and D. Ames (trans.). 1959. *Larousse Encyclopedia of Mythology.* New York, Prometheus Press.

American Heritage (Ed.). 1961. *The American Heritage Book of Indians.* New York, American Heritage Publishing Co.

Atkinson, B. 1972. "'40 dirty birds' hold their own but are never safe." Smithsonian 2(12):66-73.

Austin, O.L., Jr. 1961. *Birds of the World.* New York, Golden Press.

Bean, L.J. and T.C. Blackburn. 1976. *Native Californians: a theoretical retrospective.* Ramona, Ballena Press.

California Department of Fish and Game. 1974. "At the crossroads. A report on California's endangered and rare fish and wildlife." Sacramento.

Cowles, R.B. 1958. "Starving the condors?" California Fish and Game 44(2):175-181.

Heizer, R.F. and G.W. Hewes. 1940. "Animal ceremonialism in central California in the light of archaeology." American Anthropologist, new series, 42(4):587-603.

Heizer, R.F. and M.A. Whipple. 1971. *The California Indians, a source book.* 2nd edition. Berkeley, University of California Press.

Knowlton, F.H. 1909. *Birds of the World.* New York, Henry Holt & Co.

Rehfus, R. 1968. *California condor (Gymnogyps californianus), the Literature since 1900.* U.S. Department Interior Library, Bibliography 7A.

Schaeffer, P.P. and S.M. Ehlers (Ed.). 1977. *The California Condor—1977.* National Audubon Society, George Whittel Education Center. Tiburon.

Silverman, M. 1951. "The fabulous condor's last stand." Saturday Evening Post 223(41):36, 145-150.

Strong, W.D. 1935. *Archaeological explorations in the country of the Eastern Chumash.* Smithsonian Institution Publication 3300, Explorations and Field-Work of the Smithsonian Institution in 1934.

Torrey, B. 1913. *Field-days in California.* Boston, Houghton Mifflin Co.

Wetmore, A. 1933. "The eagle, king of birds, and his kin." National Geographic 64(1):43-95.

Wilcox, A. 1903. "The California vulture." Western Field 2(4):217-219.

INDEX

133

135